I0818127

# Praise for Angie Estes

Reading a poem by Angie Estes is like listening in on the intricate turnings and realizations of a brilliant mind, a mind that follows one path only to discover another more surprising one, a mind that observes with an acuteness and intelligence I can only envy ... But there is gravity here, as well, beneath the slipperiness of language — a sense of the profound presence of our cultural pasts, the seductiveness of image and language, the power of romantic longing, connection, and loss.

**Kevin Prufer**

Whenever I see a poem by Angie Estes I prepare myself for serious delight. Her timing and her ever-uninhibited instinct for poetic shape are the triumphs of a first-rate musical intelligence. Angie Estes is Fred Astaire and Ginger too: backwards in high heels, forward on roller skates, never have classy and sexy been better matched.

**Linda Gregerson**

This is a poetry of style, elegance, and fresh surprise, for the ear and the eye, the heart and the mind. It reminds me why I read.

**Langdon Hammer**

Neruda, Glück, Tranströmer, Bishop ... and, yes, Angie Estes, a poet who to my mind is their equal. At once propulsive and recursive, wildly erudite and supremely sensual, these are revelatory poems. Which is to say poems that delight again and again in profound and playful paradox, their mysteries both timeless and precisely occasional, as if announced in the voice of an oracle or a 10th century mystic via a battered drive-in movie speaker. Which is to say, Estes at the peak of her powers — and what powers to behold.

**Daniel Lawless**

# The Swallows Come Out

# The Swallows Come Out

Angie Estes

Selected Poems 1995 - 2025

with an introduction by Stephanie Burt

Founded in Provincetown

FIRST EDITION

Printed in the United States of America

LIBRARY OF CONGRESS RECORD

Name: Estes, Angie, author.
Title: The Swallows Come Out / Angie Estes.
Edition: First edition.
Published: Atlanta : Unbound Edition Press, 2026.

LCCN: 2025939560
LCCN Permalink: https://www.lccn.loc.gov/2025939560
ISBN: 978-1-968274-02-3 (fine softcover)

Designed by Eleanor Safe and Joseph Floresca
Printed by Bookmobile, Minneapolis, MN
Distributed by Itasca Books

123456789

Unbound Edition Press
Founded in Provincetown

# Contents

***Parole,*** **2018**

*Enchantée,* 2013

**Tryst**, 2009

*Chez Nous*, 2005

**Voice-Over**, 2002

**The Uses of Passion,** 1995

# The Swallows Come Out

# Estes's Beauties: An Introduction to the Work

What does it mean to call Angie Estes's poetry beautiful? In one sense of "beauty" all poems that work as poems, all writing we'd like to remember for its own sake, count as beautiful. In another sense, more Edmund Burke's than Elaine Scarry's, beauty in poetry can seem surprisingly rare in these difficult days: whose poems stand out as pleasingly intricate, invitingly melodious, tantalizingly smart but never confounding, founded on sinuous curves and diminutive things? Angie Estes's poems do. She not only achieves self-conscious beauty but writes about it, about why we need it, and about how it can emerge in our adult lives, our griefs, our sexual joys, our thwarted loves, and our imagined or literal travels.

Beauty in this sense — as Estes creates it — arises from elaboration, from artifice, and above all from the perception of likeness: from sounds and words that resemble one another, as the places and things in Estes's poems never stop doing. "Inside Hagia Sophia" links the Byzantine mosaics of Hagia Sophia, the mutualistic "South African birds known as / honeyguides," "signs posted // in the Paris metro" and the old telephonic "party line," first to one another, and then to Piero della Francesca's *Madonna del Parto,* the recursively fertile Virgin with another Virgin inside. Such leaps make each poem a kind of slalom course, full of switch-backs and oxbows and curves and hidden connections: they typify Estes's work, and have since her debut, *The Uses of Passion* (1995). They make her world seem — however fragile — to cohere: if everything reminds you of something else, nothing remains entirely isolate, nor forever unknown.

"I once dreamed a word entirely / Baroque," Estes confesses in "Ars Poetica," "a serpentine line of letters leaning / with the flourish of each touching the shoulder / of another." It's tempting to call Estes's own too-muchness Baroque, but given her interest in trifles, fabrics, desserts, details, serifs, curlicues and the French, we probably ought to call her, instead (as I have called her elsewhere) nearly Baroque, or rococo. As in all rococo art, tiny curly things matter ("the tail of a y swayed / below the hook") and lightheartedness can become humor in half a heartbeat: "the sound / of doves — is it *coo coo* / *coo* or *who who who?* The French // would say it's *rue rue rue,*" the sound of streets in mourning, or else "Cecilia Bartoli gargling."

Such polyglot puns begin early, in her second book, *Voice-Over* (2002): *"Hautbois, hautboy,* / *high wood, oh boy* — is that the tune / the oboe hums?" *Haut bois* means, in French, "high wood"; both *hautbois* and *hautboy* mean, and evolved into, "oboe." Estes played on the same woodwind twenty years later, in what feels like a breakup poem: "Yours is a noble bio: one note / played by an oboe: loon, loan, / loin," alongside "the i in desire" that Estes will have to leave. Any letter in any alphabet can fall under such an anagrammatic spell: "the moon has not one / iota of *I ought to,* even with its waxing tab / of IOUs," "as if *Louvre* // and *velour* had suddenly turned // into each other."

As if. Almost every page of any Estes volume contains — at least once, sometimes thrice — "like" or "as" or "as if" or "the way" (as in: A does B the way X does Y). These similes become the joints and tendons connecting the parts of her poems, whose bones are her scenes or things seen, and whose muscles are (as in all poems) moods, ways to feel: "everything ... reminds us / of something else, points / to something beyond // its own name." The clustered likes start early: see "St. Francis Preaching to the Birds." And they go on across oceans, from volume to volume, from stratospheric observations to a squirmy (or sexy) intimacy; square halos in Renaissance paintings remind Estes of picture frames, which remind her of "a framed photograph of a river / I used to fish," which reminds her of a caught trout, "looking / as if it still intended / to swim," which reminds her of how a worm on a lure would "writhe inside / my hand like a girlfriend's finger / spelling out words / on my palm." Another poem about heaven, "The House in Good Taste," discovers heights of metalepsis, four comparisons packed into nine words: "the keys of the maple turned / like parchment bats."

Things are as they are, but also become what we make of them: that's one major key to Estes's apparently flighty poems. As much as she cares about visual art and architecture, Estes has her composed ("classical") music too: melodic or contrapuntal, of course, and paradigmatically French: Satie, Ravel (though also Wagner and Mozart). Few poets today have more fun with the shapes of mere sound: "the lapis lazuli seas of Hokusai seen / from outer space, the white seam of a shoreline / at every tropical copper beach, where the long news / of the body finally breaks." Lapis lazuli, shoreline; seas, seen, seem; tropical, copper; the chiasmatic vowels and paired-up consonants in space, long, body, breaks.

It took Estes only one book to develop her similes, but two to bring out her distinctive line: interlocking, interlacing, off-balance, saving her end stops for special occasions. Line and syntax fit together not like stacked bricks or conversational exchanges or firmed-up, separate stanzas, but rather like "mortise and tenon, tongue and / groove, / tongue-in-cheek." Once she developed that sense she kept it going, knowing how it fit her spirals of simile-chasing, likeness-making thought, like the spiral stairs in "the Hôtel / Tassel in Brussels," whose steps "turn and let down their lips / to meet you," like "Leonardo's double-helix / staircase at Chateau Chambord," whose outlines finally right themselves at the end, "the way the blood keeps coming / back for another tour."

Theory-heads haven't noticed Estes yet, but they could. The linguist and literary theorist Roman Jakobson claimed that fiction proceeds according to contiguities, along what he called the axis of combination, while poetry always follows similarities, along the axis of selection. It's hard if not impossible to make these axes explain all poems, but they do fit Estes, who really does proceed along an axis of similarities: this is like that, as if it were some other thing. Stories have to stop somewhere: "What's wrong with / the past is that it's never over / and over again." Similes, however, can go on and on, outrun their banks, or run over and over, as if in an eternal present: A is like B, but B is like C, and as for C, and so on, indefinitely. "Like" and "just as" and "the way" thus recall the solder in "medieval / stained glass windows, which are mostly / broken, mending lead holding / pieces together." Without them nothing would cohere, or endure, or reach the divine.

With them all things seem possible. A lover's phone call, as if from heaven, resembles "manna, in a manner of / speaking." But the call never comes: the lover feels shipwrecked, like "Aeneas, clinging ... to the Trojan fleet." Too much Aeneas, though, would make this rococo poetry seem to sink: Estes more often chooses artists as heroes, either Renaissance masters or less pious modern designers, titans of the applied arts: Coco Chanel, Elsa Schiaparelli, or Elsie de Wolfe, the American lesbian actor who invented modern interior decor.

The poems bear their own lesbian designs. The sex in her recent work looks back to the literal lovers in bed (often gender-unspecified) from her work of the 1990s ("your tongue stuck inside me like an oar"). Elsewhere her reliance on simile speaks to the only-half-open closet, where "everything must pretend / to be what it's not." Poems devoted to ornament, detail, costume, necessarily invoke disguise, though the people here almost never deceive: they simply want more. "Who doesn't want / to be called something / other than the name / we're given?" Even when the poems do not register as Sapphic, they count (like Burke's sense of beauty) as feminine, or femme: attentive to detail and flourish and color, unapologetically sweet, avoiding practical shortcuts, hiding force behind grace. Like high femmes, they seem to flirt with their half-hidden subjects, or flirt with the reader, since "glamour is its own / allure, thrashing and / flashing, a spoon / as in spooning." The same poem compares itself and its lines to a zipper, as in Rita Hayworth's crack "I can never get a zipper / to close." The rejection of closure (as Lyn Hejinian put it) also comes in such poems as these, and in quips like Hayworth's, and in skirts, and in pants.

Some queerness inheres in Estes's whole femme project, too: like queer sex and romance, and unlike the straight kinds that lead to a baby carriage, Estes's stylish, slippery, divagating poems do not seek direct results, produce things, or justify their work on public grounds. "Feminine dress and behavior are often interpreted as 'frivolous' and 'artificial,'" as Julia Serano put it, while their "masculine counterparts" seem neutral or "natural." Defending artifice means defending the feminine too. Ornament, flourish, elaboration, for Estes, make life worth living, and need no excuses, "each *appoggiatura* / the opposite of apology," as in Bernini's St. Teresa, "pure / as butter under the painted sky." The best things in life, like butter, are something we make, not something we find.

Estes's style seems new, but this attitude may seem familiar: from Walter Pater, or from Marcel Proust. It's not hard to see Estes' overlap with Proust (whom she namechecks), nor with that polyglot Proustian, James Merrill, nor with Marianne Moore, nor with Moore's other rococo heirs (Amy Clampitt; Robyn Schiff). Gertrude Stein? Surely not, you might say, from those other comparisons; but surely so, given how Estes's earlier poems invoke Stein by name, down to the ventriloquized "Autobiography of Basket," Stein's dog. Stein's unrolling, indefatigable syntax perhaps lent Estes templates for her own divagations, and for sonic repetition amid semantic change: "a ruse / is a ruse is a ruse."

T. S. Eliot quipped that Americans could become, as no English or French or Czech person could, European. Estes (to judge by her poems) makes a good test case: someone who sees Old World beauties with an insatiable, once-deprived New World eye, as well as (it's wrong not to notice) a white woman's eye. If you want — and I do — to find Afro-diasporic, and Asian American, and other nonwhite vantage points on Europhilia and European beaux-arts, other poets await (Robin Coste Lewis; Hinemoana Baker; Monica Youn). Estes's poems have other work to do, and they seem to know that they reflect, not "universals" (whatever that means), but her particular backgrounds and points of view: high school yearbooks, suburban homes, station wagons.

You won't find a whole childhood in these pages, but you will find memories and glimpses, scenes of her youthful interest in the patterns that would guide her later flights, as when the young Angie asks the Mona Lisa, "is that a smile / or a simile?" Some poets remember the fun they had as kids, or teens: it's not clear that Estes had any. Early poems regularly, and later poems seldom, place Estes in America, in Phoenix, Manhattan, Washington, D.C., where a younger self strives for beauty that seems (to her) far away. No wonder she takes her readers on pilgrimages, not earthy like Chaucer's but interdimensional, sky-spanning and pyrotechnic like Dante's: no wonder she developed a habit of ending her poems, (as Dante did) with the word "stars."

No poet so taken with Renaissance art (or Baroque art, or sacred music, or Dante) can avoid Christianity, but Estes finds a respectful way around its dogmas. She treats it not as sacred in itself, but as a compelling set of old symbols: religion itself is "*religare,* something to bind us / back." "Mary too / had a little I am." The Annunciation and the Virgin Birth, for Estes, explain not so much the nature of God as the renewal of art, the way that our powers of making, building and admiring get passed down among generations, each emerging mysteriously from the last, as in Jorie Graham's "San Sepolcro" (an earlier poem on Francesca's Madonna del Parto that must have made an impression on the young Estes). The Passion, meanwhile, stands for the way that "Amor Ornamenti" (another Estes title) can transfigure our pain, "passementerie, ornamental / trimming" being a kind of response to "*pathos,*" "*passus,*" "suffering ... never passé."

And they do transfigure. With their false cognates, true cognates, folk etymology, and endless likeness, the poems construct for us the fleeting, sustaining illusion that sounds, and language, and our desires, not only fit one another but fit the world. Compare Wallace Stevens: "The final belief is to believe in a fiction, which you know to be a fiction, there being nothing else. The exquisite truth is to know that it is a fiction." Like Stevens, Estes knows that we're making it up. Unlike him, she gets to tool around the EU, and to give us the sense of hearing real people (not just one hyperarticulate person): the poems' spiral staircases and stained-glass windows seem to have people — paired-off lovers, pastry chefs, parents, Popes — all over, around and behind them, and they grow richer, more credible, for it. As with Venice itself in Estes's early poem *"Vedute da Tempo,"* an Estes poem, early or late, amounts not to illusion but to an enduring construction — like Venice on wooden posts: it's beautiful, fragile, made to last, artificial all the way down, and better for it, a kind of building no one can accomplish alone.

Stephanie Burt

*from*

# Last Day on Earth in the Eternal City

2025

# The Swallows Come Out

like stars, wallowing
in the dim evening light
because in the country
of blue, at times even
the borders of the heart
are the borders one needs
to leave. So I waited
at the airport, a woman beneath
a sign that said *Gate B hold*—what
Heloise and Abelard must have
been feeling when
they named their son Astrolabe,
an instrument for
determining one's position
in the universe. The room where
they met in secret was not
far from *Pont Neuf*, the "new bridge,"
which is the oldest bridge
in Paris, and like the French
grammatical liaison, it puts
something hard, something voiced
between two vowels: like the sound
you make when I am finally
inside you. It's the way
scientists knew they had discovered
a new group of blue whales: they
were singing a song no one
had ever heard.

## Inside Hagia Sophia,

above the southwest entrance, Justinian,
on the left of the Virgin in the mosaic, offers her
Hagia Sophia, which holds the mosaic. On the right,

Constantine holds out to her Constantinople, which
contains Hagia Sophia. Small African birds known as
honeyguides — skilled at locating beehives

but unable to break into them to feed — attract
humans with a call and then lead the way. For three
million years, people have opened

and emptied the hives, leaving just enough
for the birds to keep them coming back
to call again like some almost immaculate

conception or *mise-en-abîme* in which one places
a copy of an image within the image itself
to make an infinite sequence. Signs posted

in the Paris metro say *Attentif ensemble!*
reminding us to be watchful together, apparently
against the appearance of whoever is not

watchful with us. Remember when
we used to be able to call collect, sometimes
even person-to-person? And there was

a party line, not the one we'd have to
                    walk, but the one we'd listen in on: holding
the hard black receiver to the ear

was like watching della Francesca's *Madonna*
                    *del Parto* unbutton her dress only to find inside
another Madonna unbuttoning

her dress, like watching the dead flying
                    like wild geese through fog: there, not-there, there, not-
there. Not there, yet all the while you hear them.

## *Privilege for the vocabulary*

Among random entries scattered

on Galileo's shopping list for making

a telescope: something specific but not

relevant for the instrument — and by no means

something you could shop for, like Tosca's dress

which you're re-designing for a more

voluptuous soprano, just as you let out the seams

of this poem. *O reason not the need*

and *I know not seems,* but still one wants

to know what kind of thing this thing is.

Turns out it's not a song by Cole Porter

but a reminder to obtain the authorization

to publish the first dictionary, *vocabolario,*

of the Italian language: a *privilegio* attached to

the list as if it were a ledge to hold onto

or jump off of, as if just the right word, *le mot*

*juste,* could split open the heavens the way

you open beneath me and speak

rapid Russian phrases that I — a woman

stitched to Earth and one worn

language — will never know the meaning of.

## The Present

was tense, the past

was here, the air so warm and waft

you could toss it around your neck

like a scarf, like the lambs

from the island of Ouessant

off the coast of Brest — *pré-salé,*

salt meadow — fed on sea-salted grass

so that their flesh becomes tender

while their hearts are still

pumping. According to the Talmud,

it is better to wish that

you had never been born

than to think of what's above, what's

below, what's behind, what's

ahead. But still on the hills above

Ōtsuchi, on the coast of northern

Japan, with an old-fashioned black

telephone connected to nothing, nowhere,

the living make phone calls

to the dead, just as God himself

when he's alone sits way up

in the top corner "bird's nest" seats

of the Opéra Garnier in Paris — from where

he sees the stage only if he stands

and leans to the side — and sings,

*Vous me with that vous-do that you*

*do so well.*

# I Can't See the Hour,

*Non vedo l'ora,*

is what they say in

Italy when they want

to say *I can't wait*

because translation is

borrowed language at

best, and best when it

takes the advice of

Thelonius Monk: "Don't

play *everything*

(or every time) ... Some music

just imagined ... " the way

that bumblebees at

evening curl into

purple blossoms of thistle

and imagine the heat

that will stir them

in the morning and I

wake in the night next

to you and say *I can't see*

*the hour*

because the night

is *borrowed time, borrowed*

*summer:* the entire month

of September when everyone

else has gone back to

work and we go

to the Black Sea and the water

is still warm.

## *Yours truly,*

*It was the best of times, it was*

*the worst of times:* every book I had

ever read came back

to read me, along with the 474,500

migrating birds that, according to

*Birdcast,* have crossed over Champaign County

flying south, so far tonight: American Redstarts,

Swainson's Thrushes, Gray Catbirds, White-crowned

Sparrows, Rose-breasted Grosbeaks. Even now

325,500 birds are in flight at an attitude,

I mean altitude, of 1,700 feet

and a speed of 27 mph, while across the Atlantic

at Paris Fashion Week, two men waving

canisters of Fabrican's liquid fiber

circle and spray a dress onto an almost

naked model. When the white downy sheath

is complete, another woman steps forward

and shapes shoulder straps with her hands, sliding them

off the shoulders before cutting a slit

up one leg from floor to thigh. Still,

so many questions: will I love you forever

or leave you forever? And will forever be long enough

to do both? Like Huck, *I reckon I got to light out*

*for the Territory,* out where you knew the way

to my house the way a blood clot

knows the way to a heart.

## Spring

Everything is in such a

hurry, even though I'm sure

Faulkner was right when he said

*the past is never dead; it's not even*

*past.* One day the Serviceberry tree

flashes red and yellow

with Cedar Waxwings, and the next —

nothing but leaves. The squirrel

lies in a bright red halo

of blood on the asphalt, its right arm

still running, even as the halos of martyred

saints Cosmas and Damian keep

rolling with their heads

in Fra Angelico's painting. If they were in

Japan, they could be put back

together like broken pieces

of porcelain, *kintsugi,* repaired with

a thick seam of lacquer

and gold: the past could be

morning sky or evening sky, even

Evensong — golden caviar on

buttered toast — as if *Louvre*

and *velour* had suddenly turned

into each other. The past

is so unwilling to stay

where we put it that we had

to give it its own conjugated

tense, *past imperfect,* in which

no matter what may happen, the past

continues — as in *je désirais:* the condition

was never-ending.

## *Le don de la nature que je voudrais avoir:*

*Interior, Sunlight on the Floor,* a door,
a window made of four windows, each
with six panes, not counting
the panes of sunlight
on the floor. So is the painting
a tarnished gold interior or
a landscape of the French
word *hôte,* both host and guest, subject
and object — or what's in
between: the margin,
that which holds the book
together. You would
look and I'd always
be there. I would chant
my mother's favorite
sayings: *I have a sneaking suspicion,*
*That's what I thought, You'll do*
*no such thing,* and she
would appear.
Hammershoi painted room
after room, empty
or with one woman
viewed from behind, while
Hans Hartung and Anna-Eva Bergman
designed their villa in Antibes
with windows the dimensions of
paintings, white exterior walls
where light and shadow could continue
to make new designs. Hartung saved
his spattered wooden closet doors
and papered the floors in order

to preserve the overspray
because what was left over, accidental,
was as important as what was
purposeful, meant. I'd gather
all the words not used at the end
of the poem, and that would
be the poem: bespoke galore, intimate
in time, a late sun-split field.

## You Had Me at *Premier Cru,*

you had me on the hillside

of *Clos de la Croix de Pierre* in Burgundy

even though we have never

been there. You had me contemplating

the riddles of birds: *What looks open*

*and invites you in but is something you can*

*never enter?* You even had me laughing

at the jokes birds make, like the one

about the Northern Flicker that believes

the cup tattooed on his chest is half

full, when it's really half empty. You had me

at Andrei Rublev's grave, which no one

can find, although the bells keep

ringing anyway. Sitting next to you

on the bed before you left, you had me

*sitting before the road* and you had me inside

you leaving Venice, chanting with the novices

in the monastery of Grande Chartreuse: *Tu m'as*

*séduit, o Seigneur, et moi, je me suis laissé*

*séduire,* O Lord you have seduced

me, and I let myself

be seduced.

## *Le pays où je désirerais vivre:*

terra, *cara*, terroir: in the open
mouth of the wind, blue-black from all
the kites it has eaten, blown back
like the past, where the family lives
in Alexandre Dumas' *Le chevalier*
*d'Harmental: 5 rue du Temps-Perdu.*
In the about-to-bloom history
of wisteria, twisting while
the soft gray paws of pussy willow
boom suddenly above me, a thunderhead
nods like Mary at the Annunciation, recalling
how Abraham said the journey is within, from
inside us to inside us, *nous même à nous*
*même.* Where else could they be
headed in Tarkovsky's *Nostalghia* when
the chest of the Virgin Mary flies open
to release the beating doves?
Celtic *peregrini* wandered
in "thin places," sites in landscape
where the borders between
this place and some other, past
and present, feel most fragile, begin
to fray the way bison painted on walls
in the *Grotte de Niaux* move in
and out of rock as if it were
a membrane between worlds.
Out back,
the mourning dove bobbing
in the birdbath, one wing unfurled
and hoisted on its mast, doesn't even think
about sailing home. She's somewhere
between Pavlov and Pavlova.

# Because

the nodding of the goldenrod, because
the season of squirrel with a nut in its mouth
because even the green rain of the river birch
eventually rusts, because in the Blue Ridge Mountains
there were places where paths and lanes crossed
and people gathered to dance by moonlight,
because swifts sleep high above the earth, one eye
closed and half the brain asleep as they fly
above the clouds, because Leonardo said
between shadows are other shadows
and Miles Davis sometimes turned his back
to the audience while playing in order to
better hear his horn, because Giambattista Vico
said *humanitas* "comes first and properly from
*humando,* burying," because everyone's hair grows
in a spiral even the crown of my mother's head
at 94 was a hurricane heading for some coast,
because Henry James saw sheep following
a shepherd down a twisting mountain path
"like the tail of a dingy comet," because birds
navigate by the stars, because for a good while
in the night two Barred Owls keep who-ing
each other but still don't know who's
going to cook dinner, because some things
are already ruins before they crumble, I leave
you, *ma biche,* with Chanel's *comète* necklace,
inspired by the Parisian sky, its trail of diamonds
slung around your neck.

# Solstice

Towards the end
of her life, my mother kept
saying *I'm going to be here*
*as long as I'm supposed*
*to be,* as long as the days
of June and as long as
Proust said a sentence needs

to be because it contains a
complete thought, and no matter
how complex it may be, the thought
should remain intact because the shape
of the sentence is the shape
of thought: think how
the hummingbird feeds as long

as it needs to, dipping
its tongue to make the nectar tremble,
although not nearly as long as I stayed
behind the Baptist church beneath
honeysuckle when I was ten, pulling
each flower's pistil back through
its throat to drip one sweet bead

onto my tongue before my parents
drove us up into the mountains
for the all-day meeting and supper
on the ground, which always
seemed to me more like all-day
supper with cakes and pies laid out, waiting
end-to-end on picnic tables, watermelons

soaking in their galvanized tubs
of ice while the grills kept burning
until even after evening
prayer, everyone still
had mustard on their
folded hands and
faces, the nights so dark

that all the fireflies were one
giant sparkler held up to tick away
the night in their hide-and-seek
*here-I-am, over there, here, now*
*here,* as if the shorter
the days become, the longer the sentence
needs to be.

## *Ma devise:*

In the photo, my mother and aunt arrive home
from shopping to our staged scene: chairs
and tables toppled, doilies draped
on kitchen counters and lamp shades
like the melting watches in Dali's
*The Persistence of Memory.* "What
in the world?" they exclaim, stalled
at the open door in their belted
Bermuda shorts, tucked-in sleeveless
blouses, and matching hair like the tight
poodle pelt on my Tiny Tears doll,
their arms raised in the air as if we had
pointed our cap guns and yelled, "This is
a stick-up," as if they had stepped over
the threshold of heaven and found it far
more dirty and disheveled than they
had been led to believe. At dusk,
glowing red lights and posters
for aperitifs — *Amer Picon, Lillet,*
*Dubonnet*—at the entrance to the Paris Metro
guard the threshold that leads
to the underworld, although at the gate
of Dante's Hell, we're told to *Abandon*
*all hope.* My mother never heard of
Charon but always said when I
cautioned her about what she was
eating, "Something's got to carry me
away from this world." It could be
the saxophone of John Coltrane
or a *trombone,* the perfect French word

for paperclip, just as a hyphen
becomes a *trait d'union.* For Abbot Suger
in Saint-Denis, the Gothic cathedral — its gold
chalice budding rubies, emeralds, stones
of celestial blue, its windows staining
light — was a hyphen to heaven, some hymn,
hymen, haven. The iris of the eyes
in ancient statues, it's what the mantles
of the Madonnas were painted with, once
more valuable than gold. And if it was
good enough for Tutankhamen, it's good
enough for me. Still deep in the teeth
of the medieval manuscript illuminator
who always licked the tip of her
paint brush to a point, and powdered
into Cleopatra's eyeshadow: some magic
incantation in five syllables like *open*
*sesame* — or the way we said it as
kids, *open says-a-me* — that unlocks
a sealed cave, the *bon mots, mots*
*justes: lapis lazuli,* the true blue
that never fades.

## When Your Lover Leaves You

Learn a language you've never heard

Plant ginkgo trees, which will drop
all of their leaves at once

Practice the duet St. Francis sang
with a nightingale

Replace mezuzah scripture at front door
with sentence from AI computer essay: *the present,*
*like everything else, will soon come*
*to an end*

Donate matching red leather women's World Champion
Ferrari Race-to-Win jackets

Touch the clothes left in the closet
the way the ocean plays tag
with the shore, and remember her design

for Lady Macbeth's dress: one thick red drip of
blood sewn in from waist to floor

Consider the difference between *remainder*
and *reminder*, forget

how she dropped all of her clothes
at once and left them
where they fell

## Shopping List for Things Now Useless That Recall a Glorious Past

the small stones I will keep even though I no longer
remember where they came from

*artillery balls and iron or stone bowls* to grind
concave and convex lenses

a photo of the moon rising over the lagoon

*something at a distance of nine miles appears as if it is*
*only one mile away*

a song no one has heard

Galileo's shopping list for his trip to Venice:
*pieces of mirror, lenses* to make a more
powerful telescope

your words *let's not ever fight again*

the moons of Jupiter he discovered
with his new telescope

the *fur slippers and hat* that Galileo's son
has undoubtedly worn out by now

and the *ivory combs* which have lost their teeth

memory, the mast of a ship
diagonal in the sand

and Venice itself, of course — so many
bridges but which one to take

the domes of its churches still full
like breasts thrust into the morning sky

*from*

# *Parole*

2018

# *Lieu de* Moxie *Mémoire*

Blest be the swallows, wallowing<br>
in air, and the official in the Musée d'Orsay<br>
who gave me the green sticker to wear: *Droit*<br>
*de Parole.* And homage to *Montjoies* — small mounds<br>
of earth are all that's left to mark the stops made<br>
by the royal funeral cortèges traveling<br>
from Paris to Saint-Denis bearing memory's chic<br>
tabernacle of relic, *knick-knack paddywhack,*<br>
*give the dog a bone,* hinged like the thirteenth-century<br>
*Vierge Ouvrante* statue of the nursing Virgin<br>
that opens to reveal God holding Christ<br>
on the cross. Yesterday, I wondered whether<br>
there was any of my mother's fruitcake<br>
left in the freezer — then remembered that there is<br>
no freezer, no house left to hold<br>
the freezer — even though I never really<br>
liked fruitcake. In Courbet's painting, deer browse<br>
in velvet through the milieu of breeze, leisure<br>
exiles, sexier than we surmise behind their eerie<br>
resumé of *lieux-dits,* place names<br>
where lots was lost. *Ma joie?* I'm off<br>
to Arezzo to jot a note, the way Pierrot<br>
called out to the moon, "*Prête moi ta plume*<br>
*pour écrire un mot.*" But the moon has not one<br>
iota of *I ought to,* even with its waxing tab<br>
of IOUs. Held by the sky as if<br>
newborn each night, it smiles a reply, "Go ahead:<br>
in the name of Piero, of the family Francesca,<br>
and in accordance with the laws<br>
of perspective, arrest me."

# Deep Field

*Photographed over ten days in December 1995 by the Hubble Space Telescope, showing the 'deepest-ever' view of the universe.*

*He telleth the number of the stars; he calleth them*
*all by their names:* tutti-frutti, Cimabue, bracelets
of Cartier, chock full o' Giotto spilled
onto a black sky like Jujubes
during a matinee. Anna-Eva Bergman
painted *Earth Seen from the Moon*
and then painted the moon — *Grand rond*

gong in vinylique and metal leaf — as if it were
the mirror she used for viewing
her own paintings. In the cosmos
of Dante, everyone enters death
backwards, their past still
before them, just as in some funeral
processions there walks a saddled horse

without a rider, boots reversed
in the stirrups.
If speech,
as George Eliot claims, is *but broken light*
*upon the depth of the unspoken,* then *all music*
*played on the terraces of the audiences of*
*the moon* streams from the *violino,* the most prized

salami in Lombardy — made from the haunches
and shoulders of goat, deer, or chamois — shaped
like a musical instrument and carved
as a violin would be played: the paw grasped
with the left hand, the leg held firm
beneath the chin, while in the right hand
a knife slides like a rosined bow. Traditionally

accompanied by a Valtellina Superiore, Inferno
riserva, it is eaten with a bit of Bitto cheese
from the Celtic *bitu,* eternal, which can be kept
for a very long time.
The telescope showed us galaxies
so far away that their light
has been traveling toward us for most

of the history of the universe, even though
the galaxies keep moving away, just as
Augustine explained: *So I can be far from*
*glad in remembering myself*
*to have been glad, and far*
*from sad when I recall my past*
*sadness,* as in the descent

into descant or chant, the Latin
*canere:* to sing. Even now I see us
on the boat leaving Venice — you facing
forward, me looking back. You did not move
toward me yet remained in view: your face
centered, in focus, with all of Venice
receding behind you.

## *Lieu d'Hiver Mémoire*

You can find them each year
for a brief while only
in winter — a drop of red and yellow
sealing wax dashed at the end of
their stems to prevent the loss
of moisture — because the squat,
copper-russeted pears of the ancient
variety *Passe Crassane* will not ripen
on the tree no matter how long
you let them hang, as if they had taken
St. Catherine of Siena's advice
to *Make yourself a cell in your*
*own mind from which you need never*
*come out*, the way the goldfish
on late autumn evenings
circle all night, flicking
their tails in the fireplace.
What kind of pear is
sweetest? Bartlett, Seckel,
Comice? Oboe d'amore — mezzo-
soprano of the oboes — is Armagnac
brown, its mouth, a pear-shaped
opening. Autumn is so oboe,
but then winter is near, so close
to *hinter*, to *did you ever, no*
*never*, to *once I might have*
*tried. En hiver* it might
as well be *hier*, but who are
the dead of winter, are they
the same as the dead of night?

In the Lumière brothers' black
and white film, *le trottoir roulant*
carries Parisians on its rolling sidewalk
across the bridge to the Exposition
of 1900. We watch them move
toward us, though like Hamlet, they never
take a step: "If it be now, 'tis not
to come; if it be not to come, it will
be now; if it be not now, yet
it will come." Our 1955
turquoise and white Pontiac smiles
in the snow while my mother finishes
dressing for church. Stationed
in his suit and tie, my father rests
his hands on the steering wheel
as the car idles and warms,
while in the back seat, my brother
and I wait for my mother
to appear, our breath rising
like smoke signals.

## Nebbiolo

Gray patina covers the mature
grapes like fog, the way breath
from a mouth would bloom

on a mirror if the person were
alive, if the *s* of *exist* still
clouded *exit* or, as the British say,

*Way Out*. For the Greeks, utopia
could mean both a good place
and no place, just as mist

backs away so quietly you don't
even notice until it's
no longer there. *How is it,*

Augustine asked, *that I remember*
*forgetfulness?* Wine, like history,
is the work of time: what it was

in its original state, but also what time
has made of it. And what's missed
is what the French call

*personne* — either no one
or everyone. The three Fates never
missed anyone: one spun the thread

of life, one measured how long
it should be, and one decided when
to cut the thread with her shears,

just as the vintner decides in late
October when it's time to snip
the cord that dangles each cluster,

to release the scent of roses
and tar. *I don't want hints
of roses, of lilies of*

*the valley,* Coco Chanel told
her perfumer, said that instead
Chanel No. 5 should smell like *a bouquet*

*of abstract flowers.* At the end
of her life, she no longer
made sketches but cut fabric

right on the model, sometimes piercing
the skin of the woman, who had to stand
motionless for hours, smiling. At Chanel's

memorial mass in Paris, the models
in the front rows dressed in Chanel
and faux Chanel, placed

on the casket a spray of white
flowers arranged in the shape
of a tailor's shears.

## I'll Call You *This Afternoon,*

I'll call you *nowhere, now*
*here:* the cardinal's *almost almost*
*almost, quite.* Until the winter solstice
there is less light
than night. Then a whole other
manna, in a manner of
speaking. But darkness is so much
faster than light. Have you
noticed that if you go into a room
that is completely dark and flip
the switch, you see the light
enter the room but don't
see the darkness leave? At dawn
we watch the light appear
while night slips out
unseen like the tide before
it leapfrogs in. Chablis
not only rhymes with *sea*
but comes from, remembers
the sea: its chalky, stony
salinity. The best come from
grapes grown on a prehistoric
sea, limestone and clay soils
full of fossilized shells
and marine skeletons. In the Middle Ages
and Renaissance, the depiction of
the rotting body became
an art form. Sculptors carved
cadaver tombs, double-decker like
the buses in London or the bunk beds

I once argued over with
my brother: on top, the reclining
effigy of a person as he appeared
in life — clothed and sometimes praying
or reading — and on the bottom
a naked corpse laced
with worms. Ligier Richier, pupil
of Michelangelo, sculpted the *transi* —
the transition from body
to dust — of René de Chalon, still standing
in the church of Saint-Étienne: unraveled
muscles and flaps of skin
dangle from bones as he grasps
his rib cage with the right hand, his left reaching
up to hold a space that once held
his dried heart. One of Dickinson's correspondents
likened her handwriting to the fossil tracks
of birds. Where they were headed
cannot be said, so I'll call you
*what I was going to say*
*was, what I meant, I always*
*thought that* like Aeneas, clinging
to the wreckage after the Trojan fleet
has gone down: *Someday, even this*
*will be recalled with pleasure.*

## Beautiful Thinking

Each morning, before the sun rises
over the bay of Villefranche-sur-Mer
on the Côte d'Azur, cruise ships drop anchor

so that motor launches from shore
can nurse alongside. All afternoon we studied
*les structures où nous sommes l'objet,* structures

in which we are the object—*le soleil*
*me dérange, le Côte d'Azur nous manque —*
while the *pompiers* angled their Bombardiers

down to the sea, skimming its surface
like pelicans and rising, filled
with water to drop on inland, inaccessible

wildfires. Once, a swimmer was found face down
in a tree like the unfledged robin I saw
flung to the ground, rowing

its pink shoulders as if in the middle
of the butterfly stroke, rising a moment
above water. *Oiseau* is the shortest word

in French to use all five vowels: "the soul
and tie of every word," which Dante named
*auieo.* All through December, a ladybug circles

high around the kitchen walls looking for
spring, the way we search for a word that will hold
all vows and avowals: *eunoia,* Greek

for "beautiful thinking," because the world's
a magic slate, sleight of hand — now
you see it, now you don't — not exactly

a slight, although in Elizabethan English, "nothing"
was pronounced "noting." In the Bodleian library
at Oxford, letters of the alphabet hang

from the ceiling like the teats
of the wolf that suckled Romulus
and Remus, but their alibi

keeps changing, slate gray like the sea's
massage: *You were more in me than I was*
*in me ... You remained within while I*

*went outside.* Hard to say
whether it was Augustine
speaking to God or my mother

talking to me. Gulls ink the sky
with view, while waves throw themselves
on the mercy of the shore.

## *Parole*

Tonight the moon is out

on parole — no room, no light

of her own, although in the right mood

she can drag her black dress across

a continent or simply

disappear. Sometimes by the sea

I've seen her spend the night

looking at her face in the mirror.

Just try asking her to turn

the other cheek. But me and the moon,

we're like this: she says *you can do*

*anything that you want to do, but stay off*

*of my blue suede shoes.* On the *bonheur*

*du jour* of Marie Antoinette — with its *amourettes,*

petite sets of drawers above

the writing surface, and its secret

compartment — now in the boudoir

of Béatrice Ephrussi de Rothschild, overlooking

the bay from Cap Ferrat, sits Béatrice's

telephone. Her number is 166. If I had

ten bags of language, I would travel

to the four months of June and give Béatrice

a call. Astrologers say, "an eclipse may

bring news suddenly, but it takes weeks

to understand its real meaning."

Just call up the moon, ask

what she's doing tonight.

## Watching the Hale-Bopp Comet Over
## Howard Johnson Motel in Rolla, Missouri

They do not rest or come to Earth, neither
Common Swifts nor the crescent moon

in flight, but the Hale-Bopp swings near
every few thousand years, and we were out

on the hill above the parking lot, clutching
jackets and staring as we once stared

at the Indian Head test pattern on the black
and white television screen at the end

of the channel's nightly broadcast. *Do you*
*see it? Aster kometes,* Greek for long-haired

star, trails two brilliant tails, one white, one
blue because the heart of the comet holds

two immense ices completely separate

from each other. It last appeared
4,200 years ago, and a thousand or so miles

back along the highway that brought
us here, we took turns guessing who painted

the Painted Desert. After finishing *Le café*
*le soir,* van Gogh wrote to his sister that he had

painted a night that had no black in it, just
"a blue sky spangled with stars dark blue, violet,

green," stars that swoop like swallows, what
could be seen, perhaps, from the comet crossing

over us: not the *now here this* of the present
but winter's comeback, its shiver and deliver.

## *Assemblages*

after Rodin's *Female nude climbing out of a pot*

It opened with glissandi, repeated sweeps of fingers across

Keys, but like waves seen from a distance, making their way

Along the shore, the machine guns that ripped through the village

Can no longer be heard. Even the church bell lies on the floor of the

Sanctuary, tongue melted to the cheek of its mouth like the fingers

Of Thomas pressing the holes in Christ's side in order to

Believe. *Batter-batter, batter-batter,* we'd all start to chatter

When someone on the other team got up to bat. The deep red dye

Made from wild madder, when eaten, turned the bones

Of animals red, the claws and beaks of birds, too, and cloth dyed

With madder was used to wrap Egyptian mummies. By candlelight

In the Villa des Brillants, Rodin loved in the evenings to linger

With his fragments of ancient statues — hands, heads, fingers,

Arms, and feet — because they held some trace of a former

Life. He cast small nude female bodies in white clay and placed them

In antique terracotta pots: we still watch them struggle to climb out

Of the past. Before they were taken out to be executed, the women held

In Ravensbruck put on lipstick, pinched their cheeks, and arranged

Each other's hair. The women and children of Oradour-sur-Glane

Tried to escape from the village church after the Nazi soldiers shut

The doors, set fire to the building, and began to shoot. Only one

Woman escaped, broke glass and climbed out of the window behind

And above the altar, the stone altar now pitted by the rounded heads

Of bullets, niches into which you can place the tip of your forefinger as if

You were waiting at a counter, in quiet light, about to be fingerprinted.

## *La Longue Durée*

It's a far cry from *the blaze we light*
*in our time,* far from the rising
of the lights, from which eleven
persons died in London during the week
of August 15, 1665, the same period during which
three people died from grief. Nepenthe
was given to Helen of Troy to quell

her sorrows with forgetfulness. It's Ancient Greek
and like all history, *without grief,* as in
let he who is without it
win a free trip to Nepenthe
restaurant — perched on the cliffs
above the Big Sur coastline, once the home
of Orson Welles and Rita Hayworth — which offers

a quiet meal with a view.
At 5:45 on the evening of
August 27, 1783, the inhabitants of the village
of Gonesse, ten miles northeast of Paris,
saw what appeared to be the moon
descending from the sky. Some ran, some
knelt, while others pelted it with stones, chased it

down, tied it to the tail of a horse and dragged
that first hydrogen-filled balloon, launched
from the Champ de Mars,
back to Gonesse.
From the balcony, we watched
the moon rise above Cap Ferrat
because it was the brightest and nearest

moon of the year, a sequence
of sequins skimming
the sky like the lamb's-tongue
edge of prayer that rises
to an ogee arch, fingertips
pressed together. But it's too late
for Pluto, who's now planet-struck

as I was when I was
seven: my mother pressed each tight
curl of hair flat with an X
of bobby pins so that all night, sputniks
orbited my head.
High above the sea
on the crest of Cap Ferrat, Béatrice de Rothschild

built Villa Ephrussi, her fin-de-siècle
Creamsicle with its ex-voto gardens
in the shape of a ship, immune
to *bouleversement.* My mother
always asks each time
the moon appears, *how long do you think*
*it will stay?* When November's cold

snaps, the ginkgos finally give up
their leaves, but the ground beneath them
is radiant.

## Fabric

Tinsel, gauze, blew camblett
and fustian, susy and cherryderry,
calimanco, linsey-woolsey, and sprigged

lining: linen printed with red sprigs.
*It is impossible to predict what should be*
*remembered,* although mothers who left

a baby at the door of London's
Foundling Hospital in the eighteenth century
often attached a piece of fabric to

their child — "a piece of blue silk pin'd
on ye Breast" — so that they might someday
identify it. What was I asking

Santa to bring, in that photo taken
when I was six? His red sateen suit
shimmers down to the white fur cuffs

edged with lace, but his black patent leather belt
lies flat and silent. He listens as I perch
on his knee, lips unraveling their seam, a soft red

hood tied beneath my chin, grazing
the buttoned gray-brown coat. My eyes flicker
with belief: wild blackberry runners

in April, already thinking
                    in red. *The future*
          *consists only of this: that no one knows*

          *what the past will be made of next.*
On New Year's Day, 1973, Vivian Maier filmed
                    the sights seen from the train

carrying cattle to the stockyard
                    near The Stockyard Inn, where a sign flashed
          *Sirloin Steak*. The cattle jostle

          inside the yard, vultures wait, as the camera pans
overhead: an airplane glints, slides
                    through blue sky. In the final frames, a child

in a red-hooded parka with white fur trim
                    speaks to the cattle through the slats
          in the fence.

# Afterlife

We sometimes miss a story
when it ends and go on listening
to the silence that follows the final
notes of a piece of music, but at the end
of a fox hunt — by which we mean
the death of the fox — someone sounds
the mort on his horn as a formal sign of

parting. Without the passing
of time, there would be no music
or what we think of as medieval
stained glass windows, which are mostly
broken, mending lead holding
pieces together even as it cuts across
faces, bodies, and the story

they've made the way tree roots
descend through graves as if they were
varicose veins in my grandmother's
leg. After life, the question is always
what to do with what remains: peepholes
at the rood screen, where the faithful
knelt and waited for the host

to rise; epitaphs chiseled upside down
so they could be read by God;
St. William of York's smaller
but better eyes; the oarsmen in their
boat, over in the margin partway
through the Luttrell Psalter, rowing
against the tide of the text.

## Wild. Abandon

We would rise and speak with as much dawn
at the throat as the Rose-Breasted
Grosbeak, while zucchini blossoms
tested the day like starfish and you lit
the forest with beech leaves. Trees put on
the sun's jaunty cap. *Comment?*
The woman at the *marché* asks,
*Comment vous appelez-vous?* On summer days,
my mother called me home and then
served lunch on the back porch steps,
the wooden step holding my plate as I slid
my legs through the dark slot like a coin
in Reno. The mockingbird kept charging
the car door, craning its neck to
look in the mirror, just as the French
continue to ask the same question: *how*
*do I call myself?* Fireflies did not need
to be called: we cupped their glowing
bodies in our hands and kept them in jars
beside the bed to blink through
the night. The Dutch phenomenologist
Gerardus van der Leeuw claimed that rests
in music create the sense that we are
holding our breath in religious awe:
they are revelations of the holy, like stops
on an organ or a pilgrimage, or beans
making their way up a pole. That summer,
the crabapple tree bloomed twice, which means,
I'm told, it was near death. Fall
is here. Leaves are ever where, the sky
all studied with stars.

## *Lieu de Moelleux Mémoire*

"Ripeness is all," Edgar claims near the end
of *King Lear,* so what we mostly remember
and hum from Mahler's *Third Symphony*
is "I'll be seeing you
in all the old, familiar places"
because the past is precocious
like the apricot, and when it hovers
near, you can hear the *us*
in *delicious,* the refrain
of a song, a burden we'll gladly
follow just as we're lured
to *Aux Peches Normande*
in Paris by the smell
of *moelleux, gateau au*
*chocolat,* its sweet silken drift
like marrow, the tomorrow that still
lined my mother's bones
when the x-ray
of her shoulder was taken. The future
won't say *why,* won't even point
to a fork in the road, just the Y
of the doe's head, watching.
In 1641, John Wilkins suggested writing
with the juice of glow-worms
to create messages that can be read
only in the dark. Let what looms
loom until it turns into
loam, let it interrogate, enter

the earth: Read, dear, and follow
the red deer, fallow, into the
furious. Think of all the things
we'll never know — why the catbird
makes catcalls even when no one
is near, the scent of the last thing
we'll see: red apples ripening
so high, no one can reach.

## Nice Dark One

Yours is a noble bio, one note
        played by an oboe: loon, loan,
loin. Like Christ on the crucifix
                in La Sagrada Familia, encircled
by clusters of grapes dangling
        from a parasol as if he were
on the parachute ride
                at the fair, new moon, you must find
your inner vinter, rent
        a rite, a vein: nite nite.
Instead of a stone, roll
                the rhododendrons back,
back to Rhodes before the island
        arose from the sea because I am practicing
giving up the scarlet Cardinal who sits
                each morning on the feeder, cracking
a black oil sunflower seed
        with his beak or sometimes swiping
a seed and flying off to place it
                in the mouth of his peachy
mate before they both fly off
        to the neighbor's Burning Bush,
where they build their nest
                each spring. All morning
he hyperventilates like the
        rubber doll I squeezed in
my hand when I was a child, the one born
                with a metal navel

in its back, but there is never
enough wind to blow out
the low-lit candles of last year's
beech leaves still lifted
in the forest. At the close
of the evening service, they always
sang "Just As I Am" and "Let
the Lower Lights Be Burning" —
still, I am practicing
giving up evening, Brunello,
*gelato alla nocciola,* and finally, as
Zen masters urge, giving up
the i in desire. But what
will paradise be without i, the lost
paradise, the only one, Proust says,
that is true.

## *Lieu de* Living *Mémoire*

They have no close living
relatives, but because of their
ability to form aerial roots
and sprouts, ginkgo trees growing
one to two kilometers from
the spot where the atomic bomb
was dropped were among the few
living things to survive. Even now,
in autumn their fan-shaped leaves —
thousands of monks in their saffron
shifts — hold on
and wave. It's ok
to wave back, like elephants that return
repeatedly to the skeleton
of a matriarch to fondle
her tusks and bones. Once,
when a researcher played the recording
of a deceased elephant's voice,
the creatures went wild
searching for their lost relative, and the dead
elephant's daughter called for days.
In the basement I shuffle
the heavy stack of x-rays
of my mother's back, vertebrae ascending
the way the chunks of ancient
Roman columns rise, her ribs espaliered
like the branches in Taddeo Gaddi's
*Tree of Life.* I deal the thick celluloid sheets
around the room, sometimes hold them
up to the window for light,

but the ribs become transparent, the dark
between them all that's left
of sight. When we were
children, we would hold and hoist
each other up — first on knees,
then shoulders — believing if only
we could reach that bottom rung
on the telephone pole, we could keep
climbing higher and higher, the way
that ginkgo limbs, after millions of years, go on
inserting dashes into what they think
is an unending sentence.

*from*

# *Enchantée*

2013

# Per Your Request,

gilded bronze rosettes once pressed
through the Pantheon's dome like stars

filling the coffers of the sky,
and history posed especially

for you, its spree become
repose. From the Janiculum hill

across the Tiber, you watched
the aureole settle around

its nipple as if a flying saucer
nestled among the rising

stones and called it
home. Wisteria still hopes

over every wall, holding it
in place, while the lantern of Sant'Ivo

screws into the sky. When the snakes
sacred to Asclepius arrived

on Isola Tiberina, they made themselves
at home on the floors of the temple

dedicated to healing: dogs were trained
to lick and snakes to flicker

their tongues over any ailing
part of the body. You always loved

the way a crow's
*caw caw caw* hangs

in the sky like a claw,
a crowbar that pries open

the day: a posse of roses coming
to possess you.

## *I Want to Talk About You*

when starlings swell over Otmoor, east of Oxford, as the afternoon
light starts to fade. Fifty flocks of fifteen to twenty starlings, riff raff

who have spent the day foraging in fields and gardens suddenly rise
like a blanket tossed into the sky, a reveling that molts sorrows to roost

rows, roost rows to sorrows as they soar through aerial corridors and swerve
into the shape of a cowl that lengthens to a woolen scarf wrapping

and wrapping, nothing at the center but throat: thousands of single black notes
surge into a memory called *melody,* the lovers damned but driven on

by violent winds in *the cold season when starlings' wings bear them*
*along in broad and crowded ranks,* extended cadenzas to pieces that

never get played, brochure for the flared tip that begins with the tongue
and lips of the embouchure wrapping the saxophone's slurred

howl, scrawled signature of the sky. Thousands fly but never collide
in their pre-roost ritual, Dante's long list of God's works excited

raked left and right over leafless branches of trees until they
drop like the bodies of suicides, draped on thorns of the wild

thickets their cast-off souls become, unable to rise the way a wave
nearing shore will crest, something on the tip of its tongue

thrown back before it breaks and splays, starlings laid down
like the wave's rain of sand or words falling

out of a sentence: *art slings,* we called them, *grass lint, snarl gist, gnarls*
*sit.* Art slings them this way, *last grins,* art slings swell, rove

over, red rover, red rover, send *artlings* right over, *artlings*
*rove, moor to swell,* write Otmoor all over

# Colors Are Not True

although all the labels say *deep colors*
*bleed,* the way cottonwoods sometimes turn
bright red when they are struck
by lightning. According to
the legend on the excavation map
beneath the church of St. Cecilia
in Rome, there are things
that are visible, things
not visible but about whose position
we are certain, and things thought
to have existed — like Mendelssohn's *Song*
*Without Words,* which we can hear
but not sing. Before the invention
of the five-line staff, neumes
flew above the text like crows, black
marks indicating the general shape but not
the exact notes to be sung, the way
the grocery list I found in London, jotted
on the back of a map, read:

<u>Waitrose</u>
1 kg oranges
I Yeo Valley butter
½ doz. eggs
1 loaf brown bread
1 jar raspberry jam
2 real rosy red apples & 4 pretend

Even when clouds gray the sky
on a winter day in Paris, there is
as Henry James said, *a presence
in what is missing:* nuance
keeps leading me back
to *nue* until all the *if's* of Eiffel
tower me.

## History

Mallarmé said that Loie Fuller, with the wing
of her skirt, created space
like the new convertible
brought home by the neighbors
on our block: at first a question mark
in the sky, then rising above them
half a parenthesis until only
a comma was left behind, the shape
of their hands as they waved
down the street. "We ought to say a feeling
of *and*, a feeling of *if*, a feeling of
*but*, and a feeling of *by*," William James
claimed, "quite as readily as we say
a feeling of blue or a feeling
of cold," but Leonardo's double-helix
staircase at Chateau Chambord wraps
its arms around its own quiet
center, makes sure that the person going
up and the one coming down
never meet. The empty spaces, Conrad
said of maps, are the most interesting
places because they are
what will change. So was it he
who invented pinto horses, taught
the mockingbird to keep not one
but two blank patches beneath
its wings? We could hear
the car radio as they drove
away, Elvis insisting *I'll be yours*
*through all the years, 'til the end of*
*time.* From Latin *cor,*

for *heart,* to remember
in Spanish, *recordar,* means to pass
once more through the heart
the way the blood keeps coming
back for another tour, another
spin around the block. The yellow-
orange sash flapping past the window
was memorable, a memorial, so much
like an oriole or the scarf that keeps
circling the past's held
note: parked by the curb, the wisteria
was all ears, a hysteria of listening.

# Nigh Clime

Who remembers the waving hinge, how
the spine of a book or elm could limn
the locale of *gee* and *hmm* and *oh,* tingle
with the *nom* of its genome chill as if Patsy Cline
were at the helm of the angelic galleon, singing
*I'm crazy, crazy for feeling so blue.*
When the long
is gone and the curtain opens
its glee like leaves in April, we'll mingle
like scenery and ogle o'er ego and e'en, the glim
of ago.
We still come helloing up the lingo
hill, its chenille lawn aching
with echo: omen, a lien
on our line. Lean your nog
against mine own and lift the hem
of home, not inchmeal but once: your chin
on its agile cello, your leg nigh
in the niche of time.

## *Brief Encounter*

The story is *the only one*
*I can tell and the only one I can*

*never tell,* she says after she has left
her lover for the last time, in voiceover

to her husband, *the only one I can tell*
*and the only one I can never*

*tell.* "So help me with this,"
he says, "you're a poetry addict —

it's Keats: 'When I behold
upon the night's starred face

huge cloudy symbols of
a high ______' ... seven letters,

beginning with *r.*" *reading regalia*
*rosette rotunda royalty rapture I didn't think*

*such violent things could happen*
*to ordinary people,* she says, *radiant*

*raccoon, raveled rivulet raiment*
*release* although weeks ago she and her lover

sat in a dark theatre and watched the preview
of a film announced in flickering font

on the screen: *Flames of Passion — Coming*
*Shortly.* The chords of Rachmaninoff draw

dark lines across their faces, cancel
conversation like the diagonal trains

that slice the rectangular frames of film
in two as they arrive and depart

from Milford Junction station which, once
the lovers kiss, becomes a soundproof

room *reprise redwing refusal, recount rhubarb*
*reserve, reverse rustles refrain* Hurrying

home in the train she sees her face
facing her face in the window, racing

with darkened trees like the fragrant
pages of a rampant book.

# Afternoon

On the front porch, the mud cups of barn swallows
hold up the eaves, push-up bras the swallows keep
slipping into like boomerangs sliding back
to a hand. My mother taught me how to make
a fist, fingernails tucked inside, how to slip
my hand through nylon stockings
without a snag. At the street light where
someone has thrown a stone and knocked out
a corner of glass, the sparrow enters
her nest as we head into the theater
for a matinee. I knew it was time
to take a break from writing poems
when the woman at the bank asked what kind of
form I needed to have notarized, and I said *power*
*of eternity.* So let's slip into something more
comfortable, like character or your native tongue,
and then later, after dinner, we can slip out
early. But how far can the stargazer lilies walk
in their orange velvet slippers? All the way
to *Point Zéro,* the point from which all distances
are measured in France, if they are thinking of
Elizabeth Taylor in *Cat on a Hot Tin Roof,* leaning
against the door frame in her tight white
slip. The old films often flickered
and skipped, even occasionally slipped in
a blank screen. It's how the world would look
through the eye of a lizard or bird: some nictitating
membrane swept across like a curtain
at *The End* as we slip from consciousness into
*oblivion* — an act of not exactly forgiveness
but an official forgetting that precedes
what's then forgotten.

# Note

They wrote to say they'd found my mother *wondering*
*in the garage* — like entering the ethereal sphere,
I thought: *drawing near to its desire, so deeply*
*is our intellect immersed that memory*
*cannot follow after it,* as if desire were a fugitive
dye made from the blue stars of the forget-me-
not and hell could be defined as that which cannot be
forgotten, the damned condemned to go on
like Paolo and Francesca in desire but unable to
recognize what could move them so

+++

When I was a child, my mittens were attached
to each other, their cord running under
my coat from hand to hand like the blue
veins in the clear plastic Invisible
Man I assembled in the basement, and after
he left assisted living, my friend's father
kept asking, "What if my mother dies
again?" What, I thought, if she slips off
like a glove

+++

In paradise,
Dante says, we will have only a memory
of having had a memory, now lost
like the photograph of my mother's great
grandfather printed from a negative made
from a photograph of a negative, which we
Xeroxed for keeps: it's the same old
story of the Perseids, their gray hair
streaking the sky the way ethereal
is streaked by real

+++

Like denizens
of the cadenza, cicadas scratching
their cicatrices, a star shines until day
begins to lighten the sky, the shining
gone though the star remains, not
shining but not yet gone, still
moving across the heavens right up
to the moment the sky turns
sky blue.

## Dark Spots

In the late nineteenth century, some photographers

claimed not only to capture images
of loved ones from beyond

the grave but to be able to photograph memories

of the deceased, their auras still glowing
around the bereaved,

as if to capture light reflected off a body could preserve

that body over time, as Beatrice explains
the presence of the dark

spots on the moon to Dante in *Paradiso:* how

the brightness of a celestial body
reveals the angelic

gladness that quickens the body, *letizia* that shines as joy

shines through an eye. *Visit Fort*
*Courage — Take Pictures*

*of the Past,* the billboards across Arizona advised,

and at the base of the mountain in
New Mexico, a note taped

to the gasoline pump read, *Hold tight to your money — the wind*

*will carry it away.* In the snapshot of
my grandmother in her

casket, wearing the Elizabethan collar and permed

curls she never wore, my mother
gazes through her

to a planet she always knew existed but which, without

the darkness, she could never see
before. They call

some bruises *shiners* like the violet stars of the Rose of Sharon

that come out in the morning and shine
all day in their leaf-black

shade, shade carved into the yard like fish scales covering

the sarcophagus in Sant'Apollinare in
Classe near Ravenna

or the stiff, veined hands of the sycamore stretched wide

in applause, the Italian gesture
of mourning.

## *Item:*

*a beautiful hours, very well*
*and richly illuminated.* The yarzeit candle

beats its yellow heart
all night, and the next morning

the ginkgo loses all of its leaves
at once. In 185 A.D.,

Chinese astronomers witnessed
what they called a *guest star*

that appeared in the sky and lingered
for eight months, the first documented

observation of a supernova, death
of a distant star. After his mother

died, my father arrived at her house
to find only a thimble

on the windowsill, erect
as a nipple. And when he

died, I found hanging, dry stone
in his shed, a shrink-wrapped

T-bone steak. *Item:* I saw
the swallowtail butterfly pull nectar

down its throat from the bush
called *butterfly,* watched its pages flutter

on that windless day until a passing
robin snapped them shut. As if opening

a book, they'll pull back the sheet
from my chest to find, where a pair of

pink doves once blinked, two
eyebrows, raised.

## Shade

As the air full of rain takes on rainbow
hues not of its own making but reflecting
the brightness of another, so the soul
of a shade, Statius explains to Dante
in Purgatory, is made visible like flame
following the shift and flicker of
its fire: the soul imprints itself
on the surrounding air to make it
resemble, reassemble the memory
of its body, just as the six hundred foot high
sandstone walls marbled in shades of
pink, of rose and red, and sometimes
veined in cobalt blue remember
the chasm of the Siq, the city of Petra
carved in its side. Copper — from Latin *cuprum,*
"from Cyprus" — in ancient times was mined
on the island of Cyprus, and the Greek
*kutuhlpa* meant "head with wings," so the unclaimed
cremated remains of those known as
the incurably insane at Oregon State Hospital
were sealed in copper canisters and placed
in an underground vault, forgotten and flooded
for fifteen years. Mold or lichen, phosphorescent
frost? A host of ashes coats the copper: cuprite,
azurite, malachite turn to verdigris, turquoise, atoll
green and the lapis lazuli seas of Hokusai seen
from outer space, the white seam of a shoreline
at every tropical copper beach, where the long news
of the body finally breaks. Like a necklace
at the edge of saline or alkaline lakes, crust

of flour on the fingers or powder after surgical gloves
peel off, the pollen of catalpa blossoms remained
on the tips long after our fingers slid
past the purple spots and yellow flares
into each white frilly, unfurled urn:
we plucked them from the green-hearted
leaves, chanting *witches' fingers, heads*
*with wings,* our hands held up like the claws
of Hokusai's *Great Wave,* like St. Francis
receiving the stigmata or the hands
my grandmother raised when she looked up
after she had finished kneading dough.

## Ars Poetica

The shell of the papershell pecan can easily be broken
in one hand but is so thin it cannot be
written on, like the carapace
of the cicada, enclosing those hollow
abdomens that buckle their ribs
all night. We find them each morning:
notes hung by the nape
on hedges, the shape of their sound
lifted to a branch like the ex-voto
*boti,* their own life-size
wax effigies, which Florentines
in the Renaissance suspended —
as an offering or in thanks — from the vault
of Santissima Annunziata.
                                                            Leonardo sought
to reconcile the apparent contradiction
between a static, lifeless
artifact and the enlivenment
it provokes, to understand how the words of
the dead go on speaking. No one ever knew
a pecan tree to die of old age, but because
even ink drying on paper takes part
in the process of aging, he thought the life
of a work of art must be
measured by its *vivacitá,* how well
it can vivify a beholder — like Charles Ray's statue
of *Boy with Frog,* standing on the Grand Canal
in Venice, which must be protected
from assault, both day and night,
by a living person.

I once dreamed a word entirely
Baroque: a serpentine line of letters leaning
with the flourish of each touching the shoulder
of another so that one breath at the word's
beginning made them all collapse. *E spesso moiano*
*parlando,* Leonardo wrote: *we die, very often,*
*while we speak,* the way Common Swifts,
named from the Greek *without feet,* never settle
voluntarily on the ground but spend
their life, in faithful pairs from year
to year, in flight. They drink, eat, rest
and often mate on the wing: late
in the season they gather, circling in the air
above their nests, calling out
to each other as they ascend
to sleep.

## Dessert

It's what will be
set out once the table
has been cleared, from the French
verb *desservir,* to unserve or remove
what has been served. But should we use
*service à la russe,* in which one dish
follows another, or *service à la*
*française,* everything served
at once? Michelangelo's steps
to the Laurentian Library have it
both ways: they come out
to meet you like an open
package of Necco wafers, gray
licorice scent rising, or a flipbook
of the lower lip descending. While
they were reading, medieval monks
murmured, lips vibrating as if each word
were a blossom and the world
around them the amber memory
of bees. How often our own lips
have passed each other
on the street, although Bernini claims
a person's face looks most
like that person the moment before
and after he speaks. They rustle
like elves in the leaves, so the French
call them *lèvres,* the levers, lapels
of the mouth, where we lapse
into ourselves. In the Capuchin catacombs
of Palermo, the bodies of parishioners

dating far back in time
are laid in rows hung on the walls
so that ascending from the depths
of the catacombs, one sees the clothing
covering the bodies
regain its texture and color, the faces
their individual features
as if each body were entering Chaucer's
House of Fame, where all the voices
of human beings rise from the earth
and assume the shape of those
who spoke them. Like waves spreading
up the beach, their words keep
getting thinner until it seems we might
see though them, just before
they sink into sand. In Leonardo's *Mona Lisa,*
for instance: is that a smile
or a simile? Since lips
can be parted, Antony tells
the messenger, *Speak to me*
*home.* On long car trips,
I kept asking my parents, *Are we*
*there yet?* And they always
replied, *almost, nearly,*
*close.*

# Almost Autumn

and the sky this morning already a December
sky in Venice, itself a closet lit only by a seam
of remembered light. The geese send their silhouettes

across it, evidence that something moves
on the other side. For weeks in May, pecan blossoms
streaked the air and we found out

what it was like to spend an entire season
in the Perseids, how God must have felt
creating the stars in an initial O, illuminated

in a fifteenth-century manuscript in Siena. So many
stars to touch on the iPad of the night, to name
as each turned into light: *wear, were,*

*never, ere.* Down here, I've been considering
whether these split-shingle cardinals are *mottled*
or *molting* — probably more like melting

in this late August heat. Not one pecan
survived the summer, though it's better perhaps not
to have them knocking on the roof all hours

of the night. I'm trying to see what some call
*the bright side,* how the sun does not
disappear: it's just the world turning

away. In the Sienese illumination, Earth's a gnarled
green marble, the center of zero, something shot
clear through to *seen,* but who inflated

the cosmos around it, tossed it out
like a blue plastic float? I still think God may be
holding up the hem of his gown as he reaches

for *Livia, livid, ever, seem,* until a slip
of his tongue lights up *oblivion, believe.* The mourning
dove has mounted to the peak

of the roof; impossible to say which side
she is rooting for. When the sky gets dark enough
for all the stars to be seen, what we'll need

is not some pleated ocean waving
*adieu,* but a word, the last
in French films: *Fin,* what we will use

to swim away.

## Recall

She squeezed the trout until the mouth opened
like a plastic coin purse and held its hollow
in her hand, the mouth of a bottle she might

drink from, said *say ah, say a e i o u,* as she reached
her fingers down its throat, black patch, galactic
path where the hook curved like the left hook of

a comet or a hangnail of plaque snagged at the branch
of an artery, bent rod of the nibble or strike.
In *Purgatory,* God trolls his lures

through the heavens, *richiamo:* Recall the way
a lifeguard twirls his whistle, how stars spin
through space, flipping and flashing

as if they were *ricciarelli,*
cookies shaped like the almond eyes
of madonnas that keep calling me back

to Siena. *As a bird to its lure, as the bird*
*at its call.* Bachelard recalls how
the French baritone said it is impossible

to think the vowel sound *ah* without
tensing, tightening the vocal chords: *we read* ah
*and the voice is ready to sing.*

*from*

# Tryst

2009

# You Were About

to speak, like the *village perché*
of Gorbio in Provence, its houses
perched on the cliff. You were
about face, about
time, streets cobbled
with diamonds like the bodies
of birds in Lalique's
*ornament de corsage, Oiseaux*
*chanteurs,* their gold beaks opening
forever like Beatrice
in the *Paradiso,* just opening
her mouth to speak
some truth. Dante compares her
to a bird at the end of
night, waiting for the sun
to rise so that she can
go out and gather food
for her young. Each June
a procession marks
the Penitents' ritual up
through the winding lanes of
Gorbio lit only
by the light of oil lamps
made from the shells
of snails — was each soft self
better with garlic and butter?
Neither snail nor sheep, Mary too
had a little *I am,* its edge
woven so that it would not
ravel, clean selvedge of
a self like the pink hide

of the hog pressing through
the holes in the side
of the truck that transports it.
Within each shell, a light flickers
like the occasional headlight
in the eye of a passing
hog. According to Dante, everything —
*Inferno, Purgatorio,*
*Paradiso* — everything ends
with stars: like old sins
or selves, their fleece is all of white
we know, and they lead, then
follow, everywhere we go.

# Transcript

*la vérité est en marche et rien ne l'arrêtera*

ÉMILE ZOLA

Where were you on the evening of
1786, when *Agnus Dei,* the Lamb
of God in Mozart's *Coronation*
*Mass,* turned out to be the Countess
in *The Marriage of Figaro?*
She still sings *Dove sono, where*
*are those cherished moments*
*of sweetness and pleasure, where*
*have they gone,* her lips touching
then parting like the wings of
a butterfly in light that is difficult
to describe. After the cobalt blue
turns black in the transept
window, does St. Agnes go on
holding the lamb to her
chest? Sometimes the rabbits lie
so flat in the grass I can't
tell if they're there. The Countess'
shawl was paisley — once a flowering
plant in Kashmir — its overripe
comma tapping her shoulder
the way the butterfly named *comma*
lights on a sentence, breaking
its heart like Neil Sedaka's
*comma comma* in "Breaking Up
is Hard to Do." Silly you,

blessed with a sign, not dead
until pronounced, while the hawk
on the branch above
your head unlaces
a finch as if it were
a shoe. Zola said *truth*
*is on the march and nothing*
*can stop it. J'accuse*
the iris of unsheathing
its purple tip with no intention
of taking it back; I accuse them,
lop-eared after the squall, of
impersonating rabbits.

# Takeoff

Mistaken, taken for
granted: her hips rose, rose
hips. The top note, that initial overpowering
scent can be mistaken
before it fades into the heart
note, which is the final,
true scent that lingers when the purple
finches have flown away. Granted: a song is a verbal
fence, and so Delilah sings *Mon coeur*
*s'ouvre à ta voix, My heart opens*
*at your voice,* but then must cut
Samson's hair because he prefers
God to her, Miss Taken
for Granted. In Fra Angelico's painting, even the flames
of cypress flare up
along the road where the gold-haloed
heads of the martyred Saints Cosme and Damien
roll like rocks with notes
bound over their eyes. *It is a splash*
*of black in a sunny landscape,*
van Gogh said of the cypress,
*but it is one of the most interesting*
*black notes, and the most difficult*
*to hit off that I can*
*imagine.* Mistaken for granite — the skyline
of San Gimignano fallen
on its side, lines grazing out
and back like the lines of
this poem, like cows coming
home, where Italo Svevo swore

to his new wife, Livia: *I will love you*
*forever, as far as the fin de siècle*
*will allow.* He meant to be
diagonal like agony, to outlast
the flat leaves of the hollyhock, which hasten
to lace. Mistaken: the closed burgundy
whorls of the hibiscus fallen
on the path, soft and damp
as the bodies of birds. "Chicken in half-
mourning," *poulet demi-deuil,* has so many
black truffle slices slid under
its skin that it appears to be
wearing black, just as the pearl-grey
waves of moiré in the Venetian lagoon
could be the waves
of the brain: *Touch your hair*
*if you're going to the Ridotto. Nod*
*or shake your head*
*to tell me whether you plan to*
*go to the piazza,* Venetian
lovers once wrote in secret
notes that from the air
could be mistaken
for ruins along the canal where
they met: runes arching their backs
against the sea. Your plane taxis
out to the runway; in a moment it will
lift as you have so many times
beneath me.

# *Sommersonnenwende*

After vermillion curlicues

at dusk above the Alps, the span of

sky's all spick and glitter

over *spätzle mit speck* at the *gasthaus*

in Garmisch, while on the steep

black slopes surrounding

town, bonfires in the shape

of stag heads, crosses, crowns,

and hearts burn constellations

through the night. The word *spätzle*

is thought to come

from the fact that the dumplings

look like small, plump

sparrows, *spatzen,* which were responsible,

according to Sappho, for pulling

Aphrodite's chariot. Greeks and Romans

told the same stories, invoked

the same gods, changed only

the names to protect

the innocent. Although God keeps

his eye on them, by late

December, the white moons

of the pussy willow rise

from their cup of shellac into the open

beak of a sparrow: find a verb

to lacquer that, find out

what the lilac wants

whose branches hold the cardinal

in his black mask, riding

bareback into winter. Late harvest

wine from grapes picked fully

ripe is called *spätlese:* better late

than never and whatever rhymes
                    with that. *Lace:* to assail or attack, related
to *lacere,* to allure. See *delight.* To intertwine,
                    to add liquor to a beverage. Dietrich sings
*See what the boys in the backroom*
                    *will have, and give them the poison*
*they name.* In Fellini's *Intervista,* Anita Ekberg
                    and Marcello Mastroianni watch the light
flashing in darkness, watch
                    their young bodies wading black
and white in *La Dolce Vita:*
                    he lifts her and asks, *Who*
*are you, a goddess?* She turns
                    in the Trevi fountain, and the water
slipping over her body like
                    a caul bursts into a spray of buds
flung from her hips, bare
                    shoulders, lips in what the *Kamasutra* calls
*the sparrow's flutter.* Some say *spätzle* comes
                    from the Italian *spezzare,* to break
into pieces.

## *Verba Volant,*

*scripta manent:* spoken words fly
away, written ones remain, so I age
tenses like a Genesis tea, interrupted
in Ghiberti's panel of Adam and Eve
when the angel flying in to the scene
thrusts his hand out of low relief
into the apron of sky: Is. Gate
seen. From up there, the angel can see
the cheeks in *guanciale,* the rush
and *rosso* of red. Is tense, age,
all of its declensions pronounced
at once — sing eat see, sing ate
see, sign ate see, sit
age seen — while the swifts
stay aloft on boomerang wings,
calling *Gesú, Gesú,*
*Gesú.* Is agent,
see? I gate sense, said
the angel, get as in see how
the foam that arches as it disappears
above espresso becomes
each day a bridge
of sighs. Rome itself
is a get seen, an east
seeing, singe tease,
and Juno a geese saint
whose flock of geese barking
in the night saved Rome. How tense,
aegis: a siege, a siege as net, its nest
a siege, some signet ease. I get
as seen: I get a sense, ingest

ease. Unlike the night, black
and white always turning
over like the black
and white of pages turned
over and over, or the falcon hurrying
back to its glove, *nescit vox*
*missa reverti:* the word once
spoken can never be
recalled — like summer,
which the Romans called
*aestas,* a seeing set — *Too late,*
Augustine cried out
then wrote: *sero*
*te amavi, too late*
*have I loved you.*

# Via Sacra

Large forceps in one hand, scissors
in the other, my father worked in
silence: snipped off the heads
of the blind, hairless mice, curled
and bumping each other
like bees, eased their brains
into a vial. Romans
kissed each other on the eyes
as a greeting, so Septimius Severus
inscribed his name and the names of
his sons along the top
of his triumphal arch so that they
would be seen by those walking
the Via Sacra. But Septimius Severus
died and Caracalla murdered Geta, gave
orders for Geta's name to be erased
from every monument upon which
it appeared in Rome. Scrapple,
a mush of pork scraps
and cornmeal, my father explained,
is allowed to set and then is sliced
and fried, but scrabble is a game
played with words whose letters
have value. The gilded
bronze letters of Geta's name
are gone, but the holes into which
the letters were pegged
remain like the stars that anchor
constellations or the Roman tombs
in walls, *loculi,* which once held

bodies. My father built
a wooden coffin with a removable
viewing panel for my pet mouse, pressed
her into a cotton blouse and buried
the box beneath hollyhocks
and a tall white stone, the letters of
her name rising toward
the sky in *Magic Marker.*

# Gloss

My mother said that Uncle Fred had a purple
heart, the right side of his body
blown off in Italy in World War II,
and I saw reddish blue figs
dropping from the hole
in his chest, the violet litter
of the jacaranda, heard the sentence
buckle, unbuckle like a belt
before opening the way
a feed sack opens all
at once when the string is pulled
in just the right place:
the water in the corn pot
boils, someone is slapped, and summer
rain splatters as you go out
to slop the hogs. We drove home
over the Potomac while the lights spread
their tails across the water, comets
leaving comments on a blackboard
sky like the powdered sugar
medieval physicians blew
into patients' eyes to cure
their blindness. At dusk,
fish rise, their new moons
etching the water like Venn diagrams
for *Robert's Rules of Order*
surfaced at last, and I would like to
make a motion, move
to amend: point of information, point
of order. I move to amend

the amendment and want
to call the question, table
the discussion, bed
some roses, and roof the exclamation
of the Great Blue heron sliding
overhead, its feet following flight
the way a period haunts
a sentence: she said that
on the mountain where they grew
up, there were two kinds
of cherries — red heart
and black heart — both of them
sweet.

## *Wrap in Parchment and Also Pink Paper*

Towards the end
of the third millennium B.C.,
the first images of the human face
were carved on limestone
slabs, late Neolithic funerary
figures, faces with no ears or

mouth — as if, in the place they were
headed, they'd have no desire
to speak or hear, never need to
eat. Everything that delighted,
whatever could excite — beads, flint
daggers, necklaces of shells — they buried

with their corpses, saying farewell
to pleasure because they believed
the next world would be just
like this one. And so the dead were
placed in the fetal position, waiting
to unfold again, tongues held

like viatica in the mouth. What can be
translated into heaven *should be high*
*& beautiful.* Because Mina Pächter
and the women of Terezín could not
be transported out of the ghetto
in which they starved, they talked

and even argued about the correct way
to prepare food they might never eat
again — *cooking with the mouth,*
they called it — and wrote their recipes
on whatever scraps of paper
they could find: *Like strudel, fill*

*as desired. One can do everything*
*with* the body, *fill to your*
*liking,* but only what's legible
remains — like the bones
of the saints disinterred and
translated into reliquaries — while

the part that's in love with
God dissolves into *Cheap Rose Hip*
*Kisses: with the small spoon*
*make kisses on oblaten paper*
*and bake in a low oven.* What could be
carried across from Terezín was a recipe

for the end of a meal, translated
out of German: *War Dessert*
*7 boiled grated potatoes, 5-6 spoons*
*sugar, 2 spoons flour, 1 spoon cocoa,*
*2 spoons dry milk, 1 spoon [illegible],*
*1 knife point [illegible]. Bake slowly.*

## *Bourrée*

At the opening of Act II
in *Giselle,* everyone dancing is
dead or soon will be, and because
dancers pound new pointe shoes
on concrete to muffle the sound
made when they touch the floor,
the Queen of the Wilis *bourrées*
across the stage without appearing
to move her feet — like the hands
of a clock that say *six,* then *eight,*
though we never see them shift, never
hear them speak. Across the photograph,
my great-grandparents and their twelve children
arrange themselves in rows, hieroglyphs
I can't read or pronounce, although behind
them to the right is firewood they have
gathered — loosely stacked, limbs
overlapped — and my grandmother's
elbow nudges the gray sparrows bathing
in dust. St. Erkenwald discovered
the tomb of someone buried before the time
of Christ, and since the body was
incorrupt, he and the dead man discussed
whether people who lived before Christ
could be saved; when a tear from Erkenwald
fell on the body, church bells rang,
and the body withered to
dust. After her bath,
my mother would paw the white
powder with her puff, then pat

between her legs, beneath
her arms and breasts the way
a ballerina's pointe shoes strike
the stage, deer running through
duff in the forest or rain
hitting dust, on which, if your ear
is close enough, you can hear
the rain pronounced.

## *The House in Good Taste*

would be one way to think of
heaven, spacious waiting place
with mirrors cut in squares and held

in place by small rosettes
of gilt. Just beyond Versailles,
it's perfect for a tryst: lying

on taffeta pillows embroidered with *Never*
*complain, Never explain,* you can be in
and out of love the way Trieste was

in and out of Italy, making James Joyce
exclaim, *And trieste, ah trieste,*
*ate I my liver,* which, translated, means

*triste était mon livre.* My book,
too, was sad, called *Via Trieste* —
about one of the world's great

ports, a major connection between
Europe and Asia, "third entrance
of the Suez Canal," a city that no one

wanted — except Maximilian, who
just before dying in Mexico, ordered
two thousand nightingales sent

from Trieste. Like him
and Elsie de Wolfe, I believe
*in plenty of optimism and white*

*paint,* the keys of the maple turned
like parchment bats, chasing
themselves to earth, and the doves

riding their angled guy wire
up into the maple like St. John
in Giotto's *Assumption,* flying

into heaven. How many times have
you had to walk to the other side
of the store because you can't tell

which escalator's going up, which
one's already there? De Wolfe never
stopped renovating her villa outside

Versailles and left at her death
a tangled garden, the cemetery
for her dogs, each gravestone inscribed

*The One I Loved the Best.* At her first glimpse
of the Parthenon in Athens, she cried
*It's beige, my color!* She would

side with the keys of the maple, tell them
to keep their tryst with the earth, dark
and cool like theaters in the days

of continuous movies, when we would
turn to each other and say *this
is where we came in.*

# First Life of St. Francis

## I

For he was filled with love that surpasses all
understanding when he pronounced your hollyhock
name, *O wholly Lurid;* and carried away
with juleps and purest gladiolus, he seemed
like a new Manet, one from another
work of art. Therefore, whenever he would find
anything writhing, whether goddess or
*mañana,* along the waves, or in a hover of *how*
*do you do,* or on a flounce, he would pick it up
with the greatest revision and put it in a sad
or deciduous place, so that nameless loot
would not rename *there* or anything else
rain could do. One day when he was asked
by a certain bother why he so diligently
picked up writhings even of Paganini
or writhings in which there was no mercy
for nay-saying at Lourdes, he replied,
*Syllables are the litter out of which the most*
*glorious neighing of the Lord God*
*covers the earth: they burnish*
*the goldleaf lores of the white-throated*
*sparrow and lie along the highway, bob*
*on canals unmentioned but by goldfinches*
*alone, to whom belong every gondola.* And what is
no less to be admired, when he had caused
leaks and ammunition from Lethe to be
drizzled *ad libitum,* he would allow neither
*lip* nor *ladle* to be deleted, even though
they had often been placed there
by the superintendent, *in excelsis,*
or in error.

II

*The presence of worms in the odd song lyrics*
*(songs, poems, operas) is a fact: what to do*
*with this and how to interpret it?*

Because they wear a band
on the upper part of their one good
arm, like mourners, we know
that they are living, just as
a square halo tells us that
the wearer — destined to become
a saint — was alive
when the art work was
made. But as artists developed
perspective, halos were tilted, hollowed,
made transparent until da Vinci
eliminated them altogether. Some claim,
however, that halos did not disappear
but became disguised
as hats or arches: in *The Last Supper*,
above Christ's head an arch
appears, while Vermeer in the background
of his paintings hangs square
picture frames as halos. Above me
is a framed photograph of a river
I used to fish, but was it a kind
of virtue to lift a rainbow
trout from the stream, interrupt

its spurt and hurry, and slit
its silver seam — pull out
the red and blue, sometimes
a bit of green — and leave it looking
as if it still intended
to swim? I had to push
a hook into the worm's thick
girdle, feel it writhe inside
my hand like a girlfriend's finger
spelling out words
on my palm in the darkened
room during school movies. Another loop
and puncture, loop and stick, almost
knitting, until only the last inch
like the tail of a *y* swayed
below the hook. *Toward*
*little worms even, Saint Francis glowed*
*with a very great love, for he had read*
*this saying about the Savior:* "I am
a worm, not a man." *Therefore he picked them*
*up from the road and placed them*
*in a safe place, lest they be crushed*
*by the feet of the passersby.* He knew their
favorite opera, *Rigoletto,* how they
pass their soft bodies
through the earth, carving,
as they go, their own
round halos.

## III

St. Francis picked up every scrap
of writing before it went
astray, before it could
bewilder, some memorabilia
waiting like a secret
valentine: *you're my one*
*and only, keep me*
*in mind.* Every noun
and again, every noun
and then some, every now and then
some psalm in the palm
of his hand: *will perform*
*a pas de deux tonight, will*
*make do, without*
*further adieu.* To remember
is to murmur, mourn, be
mindful of things worthy
of remembrance: it could
put the fear of God
into you, but what could God
be afraid of — the no-see-ums
in *colosseum?* Remind me
of spring before wilder meant
to go astray herding
words, before the wind turns
the other cheek.

## *Nevers*

It is late on the evening of
September 25, 2006, and Cio-Cio-San
has now killed herself
for the 800th time on the stage
of the Metropolitan Opera House,
so we leap
to our feet because Ruskin
was right — we don't want
buildings merely to shelter us,
we want them also to speak:
in the narrowest house
in Paris, Abbé Prévost listened
until he heard Manon sing *Adieu,*
*notre petit table* after she had given up
love for wealth. When you move into
a new home in Japan, it is customary
to present your neighbors
with buckwheat noodles known
as *hikkoshi soba,* as if it were
the day your daughter, looking for the first
time through a calendar, comes
and asks what color
the new moon will be.
*Soba* is a homonym for *near,*
and *hikkoshi soba* a play
on words, a honeymoon meaning
*we moved near you.* Out of the blue
above Hiroshima, the cloud
was not a room for two
but a parachute, a pair of
shoes reaching for ground that continues

to deflate. *I was never*
*younger than I was in Nevers,*
says the woman in *Hiroshima*
*Mon Amour,* and her lover always
replies, *out of the thousand things*
*in your past, I choose Nevers.* Now the moon
is a missing plate, facing
each evening as if it were the telegram
my father sent my mother
in 1944 on the day before
they married, saying, *Arriving*
*tomorrow. Stop. Don't stop.*

# Tryst

*E quindi uscimmo a riveder le stelle.*

DANTE

Ancient Romans would spend the night
on Isola Tiberina, once the site of a temple
dedicated to Aesclepius, god
of medicine, and in the morning leave
a small statue of whatever had been
healed — foot, liver, eye, or heart.
Italians still drink *caffé corretto*
because they believe that in the morning
everything, even coffee, can be
corrected with grappa. Grazed by
the gold leaf of fireflies, smoke
from the lit tips of punks, after supper
on summer evenings in Keyport, New Jersey,
we sat outside on the driveway
in aluminum lawn chairs, thighs
stuck to the green plastic seat, watching it
get dark until the stars appeared in Italian
two-point type called *occhio di mosca,*
"fly's eye," used in 1878 to print Dante's
*Divine Comedy* in a 499-page volume
measuring 2⅛ inches tall and
1½ inches wide. Sweet art,
sweetheart: in *Vita Nuova,* Dante invokes
Beatrice to show how *tryst* was once
the same word as *triste,* also related to
*truce,* how close it feels

to *trust.* From the frescoed ceiling
                    in the drawing room of Dawnridge, his home
in Beverly Hills, Tony Duquette hung
                    the Venetian glass chandelier he designed:
coral arteries lifting through translucent
                    chartreuse leaves, white splayed lilies
lounging in space. When Duquette left
                    for Paris, Marlon Brando rented the house
while filming *Julius Caesar:* he loved
                    to lie on the floor at night and gaze up
at the chandelier, its glass lilies blooming
                    above him like stars.

## *Verre Églomisé*

After the grey squirrel has been
        run over, another
keeps coming back, in between passing

        cars, tugging with its teeth at the edges
of the flattened body stuck
        to asphalt outside the cemetery

of Little Washington, Virginia.
        Inside, the tombstone of a World War II
soldier is inscribed *Forward!*

        on the front and *Jamais Arrière* behind,
even though in *verre églomisé*
        gold leaf is always applied

to the backside of a glass or mirror
        so that some design
can be etched in reverse. A six-inch statue

        of a fawn once surfaced
in a shovel full of dirt from my garden, as if
        it were the first creature

to emerge fully formed from Ghiberti's *Gates*
        *of Paradise,* whereas in the catacombs of
Rome, a medallion of glass encasing

        a unique gold design
was pressed into the mortar of each grave
        when someone died, either

to mark the site or to assist the angels
    in the resurrection. The belief
is that remarkable clarity comes

    when a design is viewed
through glass, although Ghiberti was chosen
    to cast the doors of the baptistry

in Firenze because he could capture
    paradise: the past
and future are flat, what's near is high

    relief. My father's arms
were freckled like the back
    of a fawn, and beneath

his white hair ran a bristle
    of rust, which still grazes
my temples though he's been

    dead for years. Gold leaf
can't be handled directly because it sticks
    to the skin, so it must be

picked up with a gilder's tip,
    a flat brush
made from the soft hair of a squirrel.

# It is Virtually Without Thickness and Has Almost

no weight. If rubbed between forefinger
and thumb, it will fade
into nothing. If dropped, it hardly seems
to flutter downwards. If it settles
on a hard surface ruffled or folded
it can be straightened out
with a puff of breath, unwrinkling
itself like a shimmering
shaken blanket. It can be
hammered thinner and
thinner without ever
crumbling away. It can
be eaten and seems
to vanish on the tongue,
but a good translation
should have some memory
of its original language: *The statue lies*
*in a freshly excavated hole, dirt*
*and rocks tossed into*
*the bushes but robes*
*still clinging to her breasts*
*and thighs. The man standing*
*next to her, visible only*
*above the knee, has laid aside*
*his shovel: one hand rests on what's left*
*of her arm while the other brushes*
*her stone hair* once read *The past tense*
*of sit is satin and as the world*
*rolls into dusk, everything is*
*quiet except for a robin*
*breaking small pieces of light*
*in its beak: the less light, the more*
*fragrant the lilacs glow.*

*from*

# *Chez Nous*

2005

# True Confessions

*If I'd been a ranch, they would've*
*called me the Bar Nothing.*

*GILDA,* 1946

*I can never get a zipper*
*to close. Maybe that stands*
*for something, what do you think?*
I think glamour is its own
allure, thrashing and
flashing, a lure, a spoon
as in spooning, as in *l'amour*
in Scotland, where I once watched
the gorse-twisted hills unzip
to let a cold blue lake
between them. St. Augustine says
*the reason why humans behave*
*as they do is because they are*
*not living in their true*
*home.* In Rita Hayworth's
first film, for example, *Dante's Inferno*
is a failing Coney Island
concession, and Margarita Cansino
plays the part of Rita
Cansino playing herself. And the true
home of glamour, by which
I mean of course the grammar
of glamour, is Scotland
because *glamour* is a Scottish variant
of *grammar* with its rustle of moods

and desires. Which brings us back to
the zipper and why we want it
to close, each hook climbing another
the way words ascend a sentence, trying on
its silver suture like clothes. In a satin
strapless gown, Gilda slowly peeled off
her black arm-length gloves, showed
how to strip down, diagram a sentence: *Put*
*the blame on Mame, boys.* In 1946, a pin-up
of Rita Hayworth and the name *Gilda*
rode on the side of the atomic bomb
tested at Bikini Atoll; it was summer
and you could buy a record, hear the sound
of her beating heart. By her last
film, *The Wrath of God,* her hair was a burning
bush; she couldn't remember
her lines, whether it's memory or loss
we're in need of most: to remember
the way home or forget
who we are when we get there.
*Every man I have known has fallen*
*in love with Gilda and wakened*
*with me.* St. Augustine asked, *But when I love you,*
*what do I love?* He asked the earth
and the breeze, perfume, song,
flesh, the sun, the moon
and stars: *My question was the attention*
*I gave to them, and their response*
*was their beauty.*

# Paramour

An adverb by way of
love, what's par for
*l'amour* is par
for the course. Say
you're out for dinner one evening
with Yves, and you think of
the phrase *evening*
*of life.* Who doesn't want
to be called something
other than the name
we're given: the cow we call
*boeuf* or *beef* when eaten, the house
when it's lived in,
*home,* and the one we
go home with, *love.*
Lysippus, the Greek
sculptor, used to say
that his predecessors made men
as they really were, but he made them as
they appeared to be, just as Picasso
replied to those who claimed Stein
did not look like the portrait
he made: *she will.* What makes
the wine the wine, is it the grape
or the *terroir,* terror or
terrain? You think *Burgundy*
*evening,* assigned
age of light, first
sign of winter, art of
decay: *assignage,* the art of curing
cheese, *fromage,* what the French call
*feet of the angels.*

## *Rendez-Vous*

after *Bernini*

She's the *crème de la crème, la crème*
*de* God's *coeur,* pure
as butter under the painted sky,
and He, the light falling always
from an unseen source, narrowing
in gilded shafts to pierce
her heart a second time: *l'éclair*
*éclairer,* flash of lightning, pastry so light
it's *pâtisserie.* No wonder St. Teresa's
in ecstasy — is it architecture, sculpture
in the round, relief? *In my Father's house*
*are many mansions,* the many-chambered rose
*religieuse* at Ladurée, which only proves
Pascal was right — that faith in God is reasonable
because revelation can be comprehended
only by faith, which is justified
by revelation. The icing of the *religieuse*
flows like the folds of a nun's
habit, her robes let loose
like the word for
*peony,* many-chambered world
without end, each *appoggiatura*
the opposite of apology — not amenable,
without amends, no amen.

## Elegy

Think of nothing so much
as light thinking of where
it will hide when all
the bulbs have gone out,
and follow Vita Sackville-West's advice
to plant flowers you can recognize
in the dark because *elegance,*
said Madame Errazuriz, *means*
*elimination,* a room edited
to make room for more
room so that every object stands
in relief. *I have been memorizing*
*the room,* Queen Christina replied; *in the future,*
*in my memory, I shall live*
*a great deal in this room.* Inviolable,
really, like the violence,
the violins in the andante of Schubert's
fourteenth string quartet, the *v* sound,
Poe claimed, is the most
beautiful of all because it is
the sound heard in violets
and viols, although I have come
to prefer the sound of *x* because it marks
the spot in *exile* and *exit,* exquisite
and exact. Before she was
Harriet Brown, Greta Garbo
was Greta Gustafsson. Once
you were here. Now you are
the most elegant of all, the future

as we imagine it
to be: a beautiful room, vacant
except for the blonde light
flooding its face, like Garbo
staring ahead at the end
of *Queen Christina,* already
thinking of nothing, no longer
needing her director's advice.

# Portrait

From below, the pearled bowl of sky
is perfect like the belly of a trout
unslit, a room never

entered: past tense, past
time — veins filled
entirely with blue like the milk

from ewes that ripens in the limestone
caves of Cambalou — and in that room
there is no room for

memory, smeared place like the one left
by Picasso when he wiped Stein's
face from the portrait after more than eighty

sittings, saying *I can't see you anymore*
*when I look.* Then he went away and
painted it, not *a capriccio*

but by heart. What's wrong with
the past is that it's never over
and over again: the irises keep opening

into *fleurs-de-lis,* and *le désir*
and *les idées* come back
each April as *des iridées.* Alma

mater, Alma Mahler, mother of
God — who left the rose in
*rosary? Earthly Paradise, Double*

*Delight, Mister Lincoln* (color of
the scent that rose from his
chest). *Enfleurer, enfleurage, le fromage*

*des rois et le roi des fromages* — Roquefort,
a glass of Hermitage, a limestone cliff: *I like*
*a view,* Stein said, *but I like to sit*

*with my back turned to it.* Like heaven,
like *truite au bleu*
on your plate, the entire blue

face of the sky has only one
eye, which never
blinks.

# Kind of Blue

> *Because most stars were born more than six billion*
> *years ago, the average color of the universe has changed*
> *since that bluer period when there were more young stars.*
>
> THE COSMIC SPECTRUM AND THE COLOR OF THE UNIVERSE

So the universe is not blue
after all, not even green

but beige because the stars are
older than we thought. But is it

sad, even sadder than
we knew? Describe the sound

of doves — is it *coo coo*
*coo* or *who who who?* The French

would say it's *rue rue rue*
and in Italy it would be summer,

morning, already brocade,
Cecilia Bartoli gargling. And the throats

of doves, are they beautiful
or true in their blue and pink

embroidery? Young stars burn
hot and blue but those near death

are red. *Did your father believe*
*in God?* and the deer leaped

so high above the road I believed
it had been hit by a car. Dear falling

note, intention, dear
no more, dear rain,

give it up. What remains and need
not be mentioned we'll call

*what have you, musica ficta:* not
what's written down but what's

been played. What if
you paused for a minuet

instead of a minute? The dark
might sky, the blue might

star, the always
could open, the close

might earth. The doves
are just around

the corner, like a train
before it turns into

view. Miles Davis was
right: *there will be fewer*

*chords but infinite possibilities*
*as to what to do with them.* The doves

are coming, *true*
*true true.*

## Proverbs

Mortise and tenon, tongue and
groove, tongue-in-cheek, the tenor
holds the note until it dovetails
in air like the white kerchief of
the Holy Spirit tied around the neck
of God in Masaccio's *Trinity,* the dove
more banner than bird, which from
the beginning was the word for
*verb* — part sky, part earth, part
of speech expressing action, occurrence,
existence. *It is wonderful,*
Stein said, *the number of mistakes*
*a verb can make. Pardon, scusi,* word
for word, tell me whether the theory
holds and, if so, how we will
hold up, hold out, hold
on, and then I will hold you
to your promise the way the arms of God
hold up the cross, which holds up
Christ. *To have and to hold:* hold
that thought. *Besides being able to be*
*mistaken and to make mistakes*
*verbs can change to look like*
*themselves or to look*
*like something else.* The inscription above
the skeleton below Christ's feet, for example,
says the same holds
for you: *I was that which you are,*

*and what I am you will be.* So much
for *vers libre. Do you think he looks*
*like himself?* they asked, glancing toward
his casket. *In the hold,* in Masaccio's fresco,
the grave is a wall with a barrel vault
pierced through, deep chamber below
a coffered ceiling where God holds forth
in rose and black. *Behold,*
*I show you a mystery:* a ruse
is a ruse is a ruse. In Latin,
to have verve is to have
words. It could be a version,
aversion, a verse: please
advise. Not much we can know save
the redbud, which wears its heart
on its leaves.

# Cadenza

Not the unripped stitch
of the cicada or the late September
daze, maples struck with their own
good fortune, but a falling
inflection, as at the end
of a sentence or the fall of
a melody to its final
note: the cadence
of belief, something you might
give credence to if there were
a table small enough
to hold it, might feel the tightening
of piety when it has given up
its *e*. What is the difference
between ripeness and letting time
have its way? *I would as lief*
*come now as later,* as *cadence*
comes from *cadenza,* from Italian
*cadere,* to fall. *Please*
*help me, I'm falling*
*in love with you,* the song
goes, a progression of chords moving
to a close like the fall
of Rome or love — the difference
between grapes nudging each other
quietly in Puligny-Montrachet
and those grown just over
the fence, the distance between
singing in harmony and singing
off key. Memory has its own
credenza, sideboard of belief,

no legs or credentials
but moveable by definition, as all
furniture is for the French. *Creo*
*que sí, bien sûr, sur lies,* as long
as cicadas tick and narcissus
inch up and bloom
by the porch, although the house
and its porch are no longer
there, like the words
you speak or the song's
refrain, like leaf rain
you don't recognize
as rain until it falls.

# Flourish

It's the *fin de siècle*
before last, past
the lunar craze of the
Victorian age but before
the copper beech have given up
their leaves. Yew *broderie,*
hornbeam bosque, a hedged
*allée* of limbed-up trees:
the geese feeding beneath
must be stitching this world
to the next — *pied-à-terre,*
*parterre,* embroidery — the way
silk taffeta's held
close to a velvet drape
by the words *gold thread.*
Now geese hurry across
the sky like ballerinas, wings
flung back: *plissé,*
*plié.* If it were
travesty, a change of
dress, I'd call out *belong,*
*dearest, lengthening of day,*
*May until summer: tarry,*
*linger, don't be*
*long: long reign, long*
*live.*

## *Sans Serif*

It's the opposite of
Baroque, so I want
none of it — clean
and spare, like Cassius
it has that lean
and hungry look, Mercury's
clipped heels, the rag
of the body without
breath. A chorus of
alleluias, on the other
hand, is not only opulent
but copious, a cornucopia
of opinion which concludes
that opera is work, the *haute* gold
opus of the soprano, which does not
oppress yet presses against
her chest like the green glass *flacon*
*de l'opéra* held between
her breasts to keep the cognac
warm. Her notes hop
from hope to hope
like the layers of *l'opéra*
cake: Steeped in coffee syrup,
buttercream and *ganache* rising
in between, and a thin
chocolate coat slipped
over all, its name is scrolled
in glaze across the top — *l'opéra*
finished with a lick
of gold leaf.

## *Chez Nous*

we say *vive*
*la différence* between morals
and morels: the accent,
spelling, shape of the mouth
whenever it eats or
speaks. According to Sargent,
a portrait is a painting
with something wrong with
the mouth, but *chez nous*
the paintings have
no mouths and do not need
to sing because what we call
darkness darkens
in octaves.
*And indeed,*
*if we consider this beautiful*
*machine of the world,*
Palladio wrote, so much needs
oiling: the porch swing
of the chickadee's song, the mourning
dove flung up like the window's
wooden sash, the word
*rudbeckia.*
And isn't news
rude, the way
it beckons? *Le corps*
becomes a copse, someone's
opus, but we can't imagine
whose because *chez nous*
the peonies dress for dinner
like grizzlies

in their pungent
fuchsia coats while the dead
settle back and go on
discussing how to leave
a world that begins
each April to finish
its sentence with another
inch of green.
Let Marcus Aurelius go on
believing he has the last
say — you'd need to be stoic
to believe the universe
will be destroyed in a great
conflagration and then be re-formed
exactly as it was before. *Chez nous*
the world will end
like the end of Haydn's *Farewell*
*Symphony,* when all the players,
one by one, get up
from their seats and walk
offstage.

## Villa Rotonda

A classic Ionic
portico rises above the hill,
and between its two columns could be entrance or

space with a wing stretching out on each side, rapture
headed your way. Intimate, divine,
Dante's *contrapasso:*

if on this side an arch,
on that side an arch, a *loggia* here,
a *loggia* there; a wing for a wing, an eye for

an eye — but what kind of a way to build villas
is that? Palladio believed that
pediments should admit,

that harmony can be
calculated by applying the
numerical equivalents of musical

harmonies to architectural space: a post-
and-lintel, contrapuntal love like
the scent of a lily

always pulling you to
the pistil of its throat. From above,
the villa looks like soliloquy, nothing but

stairways leading up to its face, and the mouth a
round hole at the center of four bare
rooms, cross hairs in the scope.

# *Madame X*

after John Singer Sargent

What I've been
missing all these years
has little to do with
sin, nothing to do
with tax, just black
and white like the seasons
in Antarctica, either day
or night. For two months
of winter dark, the Emperor
Penguin stands in the coldest
place on earth, holding
one egg on top of its
feet, inches above
the ice, just as the bodice of the black
satin dress keeps holding Madame
X and the wolf's head lifted
in her thighs. Even the gown is missing
a strap, but not missing it sincerely
since one shoulder basks,
unkissed: the word *glacier*
before it's pronounced.
What if you call a spade
a spade? The sharp, flat
blade of the body turns
upside down and looks
like a heart cupping the edge

of where a heart would be
in a future so tense, its tents pitch
on the sea without your having
to ask, like sin with no consequence,
the mouth just opening
its lips, before syntax.

# May Some Word

Lip-printed alms! The key to rejoicing lay in the human curse,
really shocking to any who sought the mere lack
done to our racing bust, profound as a mount
but dungeon *royale* to Dómine, who forgets to
enter entirely, ill-fated *maître d'* of bourgeoning eons
without syllables, days fully fresh and forgotten,
where the key palpates and smooches, only proving lingerie
swoops deliriously low.

May some word question those, decent destiny, who
opted for *foie gras* at your surreal aunt's in August:

one pure affirming curtsy, certain hums —
ah, so taunting — the noblest aroma. Two
lay famished, important to one robed in the shape
of a word, sonorant end of brevity, elegant
like steel — and debonair, too.

Say the reigning sultan of ancient doom
pours tons of this rain on me, any song — air
invisible at the onset — may soon breeze or ante up
dunes of envy, multi-lipped. This being the case, why offer me
a calm in raw *c*'s and *a*'s, on a par, say, with a tray of tea on
ground glass? Jacques says one seems festive
if a land party craves tea on the dunes or dashes after
harmony on the loose. Elysian Fields won't mind,
I know, if I have tea on *Limoges* or a model airplane
of doom: June has proved a moving encore for your aunt to sell
the forest of the real and let June's nest pair *e*'s in the end.

# On Yellowed Velvet

*Sur du velours jauni* performance
direction from Satie's *Danse Maigre*

At ease on the lawn, the sacrificial
deer stand adjacent to the statue
of St. Francis. They are slower than
adagio, than the Basilica
of Assisi with its ceremonial
rights, but sacred and holy like the face
of the ocean, neither below
nor above. And there's nothing
artificial about them; they stand and stand
for what touches both *don't*
and *know.* What's uncanny,
*unheimlich,* in German is not
*heimlich,* secret, and certainly not *heim,*
home, which means home can't be
where the heart is but the Hôtel
Tassel in Brussels, whose staircases
turn and let down their lips
to meet you, whips unfurling
like vines. Freud said we'll know
the uncanny when surprised
by some *heimlich,* some fear or
desire we've repressed
come home, pressing
the shore like the ocean's thin

lips as they sink
into sand. What's left
when the white-tailed deer have
disappeared in the woods will be
cloven, heart-shaped
tracks. While you sit writing
at your *bonheur du jour,* the woods fill
with accent trees or, if
you prefer, eccentricities.

## Palinode

In lieu of song, *liaison:*
let the usually silent, final
consonant of a word be pronounced
when followed by a word
beginning with a vowel, and pour out
the sentiment left at the bottom
of the glass when I've finished
the *Beaune-Grèves Vigne de*
*l'Enfant Jésus,* claimed by the nuns
who once owned the vineyard to produce
wine as smooth as the Baby Jesus
in velvet pants. I meant
*sediment,* suspension not so much
willing as not disbelieved. *Blest*
*be the ties that bind,* the ties
that won't. So that's settled: let words
be the Montmorency cherries I bought
at market because the woman pronounced them
*Mount Mercy,* let them be the tumult
of memory, mute.

# Dance of Ancient Knossos

after Satie's *Gnossiennes*

Build a palace at Knossos, a labyrinth
from which there is no
escape, if you want to hear the sound
of the past, although there will be
no sound — only the home that once
held it like Satie's framed mirror
he moved to each new
place because it was "laden
with memories."

*With the tip of your thought. Postulate*

*within yourself. Step by*

*step. On the tongue.*

And keep time
at the palace of *gnosis,* knowledge; let it lean
back like recognition, legs crossing over
and over while an *ostinato* bass
holds like stones beneath a current
of notes.

*Slow. Advise yourself carefully. Arm*

*yourself*
*with clairvoyance. Alone for an instant. So that you obtain*

*a hollow.*

The river chants, looks
like a thread you could
follow — incantation without motif, "music
on one's knees," a Greek
dance performed right to
left, then left
to right, then stationary
before an altar:

*Very lost. Carry that further. Open*

*your head. Bury the sound.*

*from*

# Voice-Over

2002

## *Hors d'Oeuvre*

Have another,
*said Sister Alyssum, champion*
*of asylum* – who's missing? Who's
listening? Give me more
than religion, *le mot*
*juste, le jus d'orange.* Outside
of work, outside the ordinary
tease before a meal
begins, serve me
*canapés* with smoked
*may happen*, appetizers
seated within reach, underneath
a canopy: skirt with a roof above
the ordinary *sans* mosquitos
singing scat. When you leave
the shops in Paris, each *madame* sings
*avoir* in the key of middle
need, which sounds so much
like *au revoir*, you step back in
for *champagne* and adores,
to hear what's missed
pronounced again in conjugated
light, as if to see again
is to have.

# Entrance to an Imaginary Villa

How easily the edge
of this world becomes
the edge of the next,
the way the bedroom wall
of the Villa Fanius
at Boscoreale is a painting
of the entrance
to a villa whose third
and fourth stories hang
in verdigris air, impossible
to reach from here.
                                        Is there a room
to let, a letter
waiting, a bird who slits
the air? It could be the home
of memory, no place,
the room where Augustine
finally found God, and it hangs
in the shade with nothing
but room to grow, room
for error, which lives there as light
lives on in the cathedral
of Chartres at night. *Open*
*and close me,* Augustine prayed,
*like a vowel, like a window*
*with no view.*

But who has room
for memory with its architectural
cues: receding colonnades, aproned
stage, litany of places
all spacious and named? How close
are the cows coming home
from the field? How near
are the birds not
singing? Neither high nor low
relief can be found on the terraced
paths the cows have worn
across the hills for centuries. Flat
as literal translation, something roams
around its rising rooms, repeating
*O*'s and making vows to slide
the window close
to closed, to hear the wind
first low then rise
like the chickadee's
song, all vowels.

# Scripture

I'll tell you what is meant
on condition that it be
understood, what is lent on condition
that it be returned. Chartreuse,
first ruse of spring, liqueur
of the Carthusian monks at Grenoble,
is pale green, yellow as eggs

inside fresh hens in the markets
of Firenze each spring, pale
as the grappa from Piemonte
whose label, handwritten in red
and black ink on torn
paper reads *Dear Maria,*
*I have to talk to you.*

Le Corbusier's statue of Mary
in the chapel at Ronchamp
swivels to bless pilgrims inside
and out, but the effigy Ruskin found
on the tomb he climbed
in Santi Giovanni e Paolo
turned out to be only half

a Venetian doge: one hand, one
cheek, one side of the forehead
wrinkled, carved to be seen only
from below like the face
of the moon we can see
or the cameo, raised relief
of love. What is lent:

the curved throat
of the road, the deer
thrown back like the *s*
in *swan:* squirrel
flat on the asphalt, carnival
mask, its own black map
of what it means.

# Now and Again: An Autobiography of Basket

for Gertrude Stein

Comets are like scythes, they do not hold
your coat, although they may look
as if they are going to, just rounding
the corner into the century, but perhaps she was
speaking of commas, celestial bodies trailing
bright hair every seventy some years,
once through a lifetime if you're lucky
you see them, two women and a poodle
curved into hummocks, asleep
and slung between sheets, still now
and again her mouth would open,
grin, and then bear down
on something it looked like dahlias
she carried in her teeth and time
and time again it was my name,
so sometimes we danced, my paws
on her shoulders in the garden of Bilignin
while she sang *I am I because my little dog*
*knows me* to the tune of "On the Trail
of the Lonesome Pine," *each part needing its own*
*place to make its own balancing*
as in a sentence she said, there is a mirror
of that and another photo, too,

where we sit as we were told to
on the sofa in front of the portrait
she painted me on the wall behind, when time
and time again she told me to sit
because she loves me in that painting
she says there I am God's dog, ASCOB,
who barks all the time but is impossible
to hear, that *my* epitaph, too, should declare
*Any Solid Color Other than Black*
when the time comes to call
everything back to where it belongs,
to its place in some long sentence
where I was going to say we are
the commas, tipped like hammocks
in the wind, but then again now
I think, rather, we are the hammocks
in which the commas swing.

# Rhapsody

No one says it
anymore, *my darling,*
not to the green leaves
in March, not to the stars
backing up each night, certainly
not in the nest
of rapture, who
in the beginning was
an owl, rustling
just after silence, whose
very presence drew
a mob of birds — flickers,
finches, chickadees, five cardinals
to a tree — the way a word
excites its meanings. *Who*
*cooks for you,* it calls, *Who looks*
*for you?* Sheaf of feathers, chief
of bone, the owl stands
upon the branch, but does he
understand it, think *my revel,*
*my banquet, my tumult,*
*delight?* The Irish have a word
for what can't be
replaced: *mavourneen, my*
*darling,* second cousin once
removed of memory, *what is not*
*forgotten,* as truth was

defined by the Greeks.
It's the names
on the stones in the cemetery
that ring out like rungs
on a ladder or the past
tense of bells: Nathaniel Joy,
Elizabeth Joy, Amos
Joy and Wilder Joy,
and it all comes down
to the conclusion
of the cardinal: *pretty, pretty, pretty*
*pretty* — but pretty what?
In her strip search
of scripture, St. Teresa
was seized, *my darling,* rapt
amid the chatter
and flutter of well-coiffed
words, the owl
in the shagbark hickory,
and all the attending dangers
like physicians
of the heard.

# Classical Order

sheep horns curled at the head, limestone
head of Dionysus, acanthus leaves
finishing their upward crawl, licking
their tongues, beginning to curl —
violin scroll in high relief, wig rolled
just to the ear   *whether there be tongues,*

*they shall cease*   antique
silent to the eye
without taper and flute, wick
to what light, narrowed but not
diminished, perhaps diminished
but arriving at an end
and, thus, without perspective

high-pitched instrument, reedless
mouthpiece at the end, long
parallel grooves incised
on the shaft of the column —
pleated ruffle, tutu

but placed on earth, touching base
with a dewclaw,
something vestigial we carry
with us, reaching only
the dewy surface of the ground

*something to turn on,* then,
capital: Corinthian    column: spinal
and never plumb
with anything, segmented
stack of sobriquets,

vertebrae, from *vertere,* to turn
*something to turn on*
hereafter nicknamed Veronica
*verus iconicus*
whose handkerchief
preserves the true image

of a face, cape
passed slowly before
a charging bull
while the matador stands
immobile   *though I speak*

*with the tongues*
*of men and of angels*   consider
the pilasters that assist at the mouths
of mausoleums, think
of all the motel rooms across America
that do not want
to be disturbed

## Vermeer Fever

*Scientists for the first time have used a natural chemical to dramatically increase the life spans of human cells in laboratory dishes and perhaps make them immortal.*

THE WASHINGTON POST, January 14, 1998

We all came down with it
in the seventeenth century, back

when it was still possible
to die. It was necessary then

to dwell on drops of rain
until all the world

wore beads, as when Vermeer, for instance,
made entire landscapes inlaid

with pearl, brass chandeliers
beaded, brick houses mortared

with pearl — and not just the necks
of women, either, but seed pearled boats,

bridges, cold silver pitchers, rivers
and ribbons and bread; of course

in some paintings, even pearls
and paintings, too, eventually came down

with Vermeer fever — beyond our reach
to cure, the way the shape

of light resembling a pearl
could be conjugated

into *passé composé* and finally
turn into light. We were like

the squirrel, high on a branch
in winter, who curves his tail forward

to cover his body and become
the initial that stands

for his name; we, too, were diagnosed,
admitted: *Je me ressemble,*

*I resemble no one*
*so much as myself.*

So many tapestries lifted,
pulled back; on every wall

a map. So many paintings
covered with glass

to ward off the fingers
of unbelievers. She has no place

among us now, that woman
Vermeer once drew in fever,

eye and earring inviting us in.
She will go on turning toward us,

turning away —
the way the black and white

of water and ice swirl around
each other in a January stream —

but like lilacs that no longer
bloom without the hold

of winter, we have no need
of necklaces, glances,

or desire. Full moon turning back
to a darkened place, she can keep

the prognosis that love
must always have.

# *Amor Ornamenti*

It is easier to love beautiful
*creatures, sweet scents, and lovely*
*sounds than to love*
*God,* the eighth-century scholar
Alcuin said, so God invented
passementerie, ornamental
trimming for curtains, pillows,
and gowns — gold braid, silver
beads, the silk-and-gilt
tinsel of passion, translated
from the Greek *pathos* from Latin
*passus: suffering, to suffer* —
never passé, never out of
fashion. Howling human, winged
monster, lion-headed
body projecting from a gutter
to carry rainwater clear
of the wall: gargoyle —
as in *guttur, gargoul,* as in
gutter, in throat — narrow stony
astonished passage — liaison
to what? And where is syntax,
sentence, *my liege,* which leads to
sacrilege, the stealing
of sacred things? The presentation
and movement of the cape to
attract, receive
and direct the charge of

the bull is called
*pase.* The Indian name for
the buckeye tree: *hetuck,*
"eye of the buck," for the glossy
brown orbs that split
their green lids like seams.

## Narrative

The colonnades on St. Peter's Square
embraced Bernini's ellipse and many stories
beneath me was Rome, its own
*roman à clef,* home of
the Pantheon of Marcus Agrippa, built
under the Pantheon of Hadrian
where Raphael was later
buried: shell of a turtle, no place
with entrance and light
placed at the center
of its coffered dome: *
little star, asterisk, unattested
existence not established by documentary
evidence, but reliably inferred
*see *hole* *see *light*
*see *shape* of the space made
by music, a room
we can hear: pierced ceiling
that will miss the dark, which was
so clear and clever.

## *Roma Caput Mundi*

Their place is now taken
*by ruins, but not by ruins*
*of themselves but of later*
*restorations,* Freud said
of the Senate and People of
Rome — otherwise known
as *SPQR,* inscribed
above the arch of Septimius Severus:
Senatus Populus Que Romanus
Silk Pajamas Quietly Rule Us
*Seven Peaches Quite Ripe*
*Some Passing Qualm Resurfaced*
*Some Private Quarrel Revived*
*Same Palatial Quiz Revisited*
Some Possible Quiet Remains
                                        At the place
where three roads met, ancient
Romans posted news: *trivia*
they called it, for the way
that all roads lead only
*to roam* until we end up
at memory and find not
what we left there
but the history of how we wanted it
to be. We might as well call
the fine line finishing off
each letter of Roman type
*seraph,* the peonies lifting
up from the loam
and the sheaves of hosannas
we call hostas, *Romans,*
every one, rising from the
ruins of what we've become.

# History

Since every work of history omits
more than it includes, one must
choose what mattered most, use
Michelangelo's art of subtraction
to take away every word
that is not the poem. Keep the gold
*fleurs-de-lis* and the *coeurs*
*de lion,* lit (as with light)
or *lit* as in lying in their French
bed of blue. Keep the statue
from Samothrace but say *adieu*
to her view, and keep August
so that goldfinches will finally
mate and there will be purple
and white thistledown to line
their nests. Since whatever color
we can see is the only color
an object's not, fill up the poem
with blue and let it try each day
like the ocean to turn itself
into what it is not. Then love
the poem as the poem
loves the color blue and end
as Italians do after
a long meal, with something bitter, *amaro,*
or searing, a *grappa.*

## The Annunciation in an Initial R

But whose initial? Left here, illuminated
        but abandoned by its text. Surely *R* stands
for religion, *religare,* something to bind us
        back, to remind that — whether reading, kneeling,
or waving goodbye — a word can enter
        our womb in a breath. Bordered with heads,
each open mouth tongued orange or blue
        with the tip of a pen, the letter *R* could be
autumn, all parchment and loss, each leaf
        embedded with flame.

More like *enunciation,* I should think,
        with the lungs a heavy butterfly heaving
its cocoon, and the conception some act
        of ventriloquism, immaculate and marooned.
Perhaps *R* is for rental — as in the villa
        where they sit, Mary and Gabriel tilting
their heads. And the gold leaf rolling in
        wherever space remains is nothing
but time, in which everything floats. Is this the way
        rooms imagine us to be: round-shouldered
and arched, all presence and tense, waiting
        for words to arrive in our ear? Space
now fulfilled, place where bulbs are forced
        to bloom — like skulls without thoughts, are they empty
without us? Initials can begin

or put an end to a name, tell stories,
    train vines, and use the bodies of others
to form their own shape; jungle gyms
    of intention, designed to mean
*this one and not another,* initials took the place
    of people, already replaced
by words, until they finally took over
    the page and made everything
in their image. Anthropomorphic, historiated, foliate:
    they became, like us, inhabited.

If *R* is for annunciation, then *T* can signal
    crucifixion: cross illuminated, tipped
on its side, cartwheeling to Golgotha,
    where *X* marks the spot. *Te igitur,* You therefore,
*clementissime Pater, per Jesum Christum Filium tuum Dominum nostrum,*
    *supplices rogamus, ac petimus*
the priest chants, arms and palms espaliered
    at his sides. Slowly lowered, the hands meet
again, cupping each other the way Adam and Eve
    hid from God their most private
parts, the parts he could not bear
    to see. Like flags waved by sailors
from decks of separate ships, their hands
    made the semaphore which means
        *end of word.*

## *Vedute da Tempo*

This time of year, even birds have stars
in their eyes, traveling north
by night; one true far place holds
the dart of their gaze as we fly
over Manhattan. Of all the fires
that slowly turn below, a single lamp
beside a bed is the only star
to which we want to go, out of all
the faces in the airport crowd,
only one will do.

The wise men knew why we want
to flee — first away from, then toward —
whatever bright thing may wink
in the sky. Like Lazuli Buntings,
they offered up wings and found their way
to *what remained of what used*
*to be* — and other spent words
for *home:* is that where they were
in the north or the south, in winter
or in spring? They knew, before Lacan,

the reason we travel: *one is the image of oneself*
*with which one tries, like a perpetual child,*
*to catch up.* And if misrecognition of some other
in the mirror indeed produces a self,
where better than Venice
for *méconnaissance:* damask city
of the milk-breasted goddess, coiffure
plaited in gold, city of so many men found
in female dress, a law had to be passed

against it, courtesans forbidden to parade

in boats, courting men while clothed
in the clothing of men. Mirror held up
to its own waving image, city that could lose
the library of Petrarch and not even miss it
for a hundred years, busy posing
for another of Canaletto's views: Ca' d'Oro,
Ca' Rezzonico, reflection of St. Mark's
facade, all repeat the ancient Venetian motto,
*Vedute da Tempo — reflect, refract,*

*and float.* To begin with, nothing
of its own — but clever, adaptable, rising
on piles driven into silt, tongue
bobbing in the mouth like a boat. Now the black
beaked gondola we've hired for the night
strokes the water with its one pale wing,
cleaving canals into left and right, light
and shade, formless
then made; like antlers pushing
from the skull each May, the oar

touches something finally called *bottom,*
cuts velvet, and takes us back
the way we came. Stepping from the boat
to the stones of the street, at what point
can we say we have been
to *Venice?* The word itself
wears silk brocade — is flowing, loose,
unnavigable — but stars still bloom
across it each night, watch themselves lit
by some dark lagoon.

# *Trompe l'Oeil*

Zeuxis painted grapes so real
that birds came down
to peck, but Parrhasius painted
a curtain that Zeuxis asked him to
pull back.
                    What is a curtain
but a promise that something lies
behind it, nothing
but definition, burgundy
velvet, draped. But *Why a little curtain*
*of flesh on the bed of our*
*desire?* Blake never tired of
asking, though Pliny had already
decreed that the best
painting of all would be
a painting of a curtain
since paintings should *disclose*
*even what they hide.*
                              Around 500 BC
some Greek no longer believed
everything he saw
needed to be
shown, but only the angle
from which it is seen: a back
too short from neck to
waist, backing out of
a frame, would mean
*grief;* head next to shoulder, cheek
on knee could say *bent* or
*let's see* — the stage built

in perspective

                                        at Teatro Olimpico

in Vicenza might be a stage

for love, streets narrowing

to a place where it looks as if

we could walk forever.

# More

arch than sky, more vault
than heaven, roof
of the mouth, more tent
than motet covering the space between
notes. *Hautbois, hautboy,*
*high wood, oh boy* — is that the tune
the oboe hums? Above
the nave, triforium, clerestory,
vault, every arch points
to what? Architecture
is the building
of interior space: a cathedral, a glove
for the hand of God, gladiolus,
foxglove ascending as if
there's no end. What then? Music
is what is left of lustre, heading
west: the shape of what's spread
between the ceiling's
ribs, vaulted beaks
of how many birds in the nest
asking for

*from*

# The Uses of Passion

1995

## A Poem Called Lost at Sea

I always wanted to write a poem called lost at sea
Complete with fore and aft and masts
And rigging, sails I could inflate
Like cherubic cheeks of laundry, hoisting
Them off into oblivion.

Then after heaving in fog for days,
I and whatever reader remained would lift
Our heads as we rolled into imagery deep
And blue, dipping our faces overboard
Into its dark, swirling skirt.

All at once the sea would be personified
And come to resemble every lover
I ever knew. In the panic that followed,
Line breaks of any kind would be forbidden;
Everyone who threatened mutiny

Would be chained in the hold, and anyone caught
On deck without permission — my mother, for instance —
Could argue her view from the gangplank
While I lay on the tip of the bow, adjusting
The height of the horizon.

The irony of the poem would be that no one would ever
Cry out "Land ho!" because, of course,
We were lost at sea, tacking carelessly
Across the hips of the ocean, and it was night,
And as in all good poems, in the depths lurked

Hidden meaning. One day, sun-rotted, the sails
Would mercifully unzip, and the naked lines of a poem
Called "Lost at Sea" could finally suggest
What happened: How your tongue stuck inside me like an oar,
How you and your boat kept turning, turning, turning.

# The Classical Tradition

The most distinctive feature of the classical
tradition is that the nose
is always the first
to go: nicked by the chisel
of its own impassioned sculptor
stepping quickly back from another

perfect piece. When the bodies
of ancients were turned
into stone, some limbs always
refused to remain; lifted to pedestals
at courtyard gates, the arms slipped
quietly off in an admirer's hand.

Nor could classical figures be carried
into rooms: grasped
about the thighs and vaulted
inside, their heads
dropped off like plums
suddenly ripe and amazed.

It's how we always recognize
antiquity: perfected, smooth
and cool to the cheek, our own
rounded bodies pushed into light,
broken and waiting to be touched.

# Perspective

It was the Renaissance talk
of the town: the shoulders of painters
tapped each other like pearls
on a necklace, heads drawn together
toward some not understood yet inevitable point
above the drawings before them.

We too have watched it in gardens
angling the bean rows to the center gate.
This is the spot on which we have gazed
as a lover moons into space, the target
we wanted all our arrows to hit.
Should it rise even now above us
like death, its empty disk
would drag our eyes like skirts
through the sky, though we've seen
each evening how all the sun's rays
look back to the sun and then go blind.

Once you've waited out the heart's two-step
finish, you know what the blood
has had to know all along:
that the heart is hollow, holds nothing
of its own. Always the limber years
will chase you down the street,
stopping abruptly behind you —
one hand held lightly in the small
of your back, the other pointing ahead
in some narrow direction.

# *St. Francis Preaching to the Birds*

after Giotto

At first I thought he was feeding them,
fingers just released above their heads,
until I saw how they held their beaks tight
and final, as if they had made up their minds
never to eat or love again. Of course
it's another of his pantomimes, and no one

in the painting speaks, although the thrush, grouse,
and one other kind of bird I can't quite
make out, lift and tilt their heads
as if they had looked up in the middle
of reading to consider
what they had just taken in, anticipating

what is to come. So far, only one thing reaches
toward heaven, a tree whose spine curves
behind them like a comma, and in the space it frames
at the center of the painting is a pause
on which an evening grosbeak and a pigeon
still intend to land. What does it mean

to say the dead no longer exist; is it the same
as saying that love, when it's over,
is gone? If this were a parable
of love, St. Francis would swing that arm
forward and send them all slapping
in flight; they would see they could choose

to stay just as they are — Scrub Jay, Steller's Jay,
and Clark's Nutcracker, each faithful
in its own gregarious niche, the Red-breasted Nuthatch
clutching its Russian *nyet* — even as we
could stop right here and refuse to go on
to another word, refuse to have

the word we long to hear become a bit
in the mouth while the mouth is still tender.
I hope it's not a lesson in love, with the tree
stroked in on the side like a prop, while the fingers
of St. Francis and the two birds splayed
in flight keep trying to touch

what can never be there. I prefer to think
that before he happened by, they were pecking
at words on a page just turned over
into light, that they had lifted some shape
of ink they could not swallow. St. Francis drew them
a picture of the hole in the ground

where what was once the ground
used to be, and without speaking a word
before he turned to leave said, *Let us*
*pray to this place that is not*
*a place, let the three toes*
*of this tree hold on*

*while the gold flecks of the sky*
*peel back; let us believe that we can say*
*what it will be like to stay put:*
*at first a flock of Bushtits, nipping*
*at the heart; then overhead,*
*the unaccountable stars.*

## Serenade

Yelling never works, but I'm told
that sometimes
a well-pitched shoe
or the unusually stiff
beam of an ardent flashlight
will get them
to move on.
I hear them warming up
each evening about five,
while wooden spoons
turn around in their pots.
After he has chased
the intruder away
from the car door's mirror, flashing
the blankness held beneath wings,
the mockingbird begins
to repeat everything he has ever heard
you say: how it is time
to get to the table,
how there will be seconds
for all, how at the beginning
of June you are willing to pay
six times the going price
for a basket of tomatoes that you will want
to give away at the end
of July.

When all the words that could be said
had been, when all
the verbs that could be moved
were, the mockingbird had to be
invented to remind us to be sure
to remember
everything we had wanted
to forget. So mockingbirds sing
the same songs each year,
although some are sung once
and never repeated
because if, in repeating, a wrong note
is sung, mockingbirds know
like musicians
or lovers, to sing it again
so you think
that they meant it, to keep
doing it over
until they get it right.
And while they go on believing
that what's repeated long enough
does become
right, you lie awake imagining
sleep, how it will arrive
at last with the thick, humid scent
that remains
when the house is empty of everything
but darkness, and one
oblong bud of gardenia
spreads its thickened cream.

In the wide hour
before dawn, the bird calls
and raises, convinced
that the heart's full
deck has been played,
that a flush
beats a straight,
or two of a kind,
nothing,
but before sleep moves in
like the final bet
to be placed, the heart's tattoo
doubles, coaxed on
by what remains: memory's cadenza
of roses
that go one climbing in the absence
of any frame, absence
dragged in and out
of the beak
like song.

# Reply

## I

Sticks can urge most anything on
with their drum rolls of incantation.
Painted and sharpened, they quicken
our vision—a white cane,
a poke in the eye. Their power
is in their thighs: A simple cross
of the legs and there's a crucifix
or a fire, but sticks are not at all
good witnesses; they burn quickly
and can be frightened into stone.

Some have no interest in stiffening: the willow
stays busy praising the earth, stroking and washing
the brown feet with its hair, calling
it sweet names like *Jesus*.

## II

The common stones we walk on
are descendants of the molars of Demosthenes
grinding themselves over the centuries to dust.
They know everything there is to know
about falling in love
but can say nothing of it.

Boulders are wiser: they worship their own
gray monolithic hips. Often we stumble
upon them basking in their great surprise.
Theirs is the silence of double agents;
in their other life, they are words.

## III

Some say that words outlive us, as if
you could somehow know
mine by their little blue eyes. It's the same
problem with birth: what to do with what now
resembles you, and even worse, what to call it.
Best to wrap it in bailing wire and wait
for something that will cock
the dog's ear.

Some of us have no name and so never answer
when called—a weed, a spade, a poem.
It's like having something in common with God:
whatever you can imagine,
we're not.

# Resolutions for a New Year

Whatever's left in November: whatever unfinished mounds
beside a rake, whatever leaves unconvinced

to mulch, whatever earthworms meandering through loam
below branches grown to just here and no farther,

no matter whether we dash outside in time
to see the geese wagging their gray crepe ribbons

against the sky, nothing, nothing will remind
us of desire. Whatever we can hold

between forefinger and thumb, whatever
tight white knots we can press

in the measure of our own hand,
we will shove away from us into the dark

holes of the earth reserved
for the stalled hearts of bulbs.

But whatever the ground dreams up
by the time we've noticed

it's spring, we will bundle
in our arms and usher

to the house, though the tulips
look back to the garden

when we're gone, their necks
unruly as loss.

## The Dance of the Sheets

for my mother

After do-si-doing all those years
the steps are learned at last
steps we practiced over and over
out back
under the clothesline
you in white boots
indivisible from the glittering snow
as you whipped away
yet another bleached sheet
to hang in front of my frozen eyes.

On this at least we finally agree —
that it's left over right
shake and turn
fold in the middle.
And as I approach you now
corner to corner
eye to eye
I lower myself to
myself
on this white gleaming mirror
arms outstretched, a blinded lover
amazed
that we dance
together.

## Apples in August

Someone on the other side of the fence
is beating tree branches with a stick,

knocking the yellow apples from their boughs.
I suppose that's how you know

they are ripe, when they no longer
need coaxing and drop to the ground

with aplomb, bouncing — at most —
only once. But I've seen some

yanked off with a twist, their limbs
sprung upright and dazed

as the dead will rise up, when the lights
click on, the morning of Judgment Day.

The apples I like best stay on the tree
and wait, although I've heard them stumble

to the ground at night when they think
that no one is near. Of the ones

that remain, most will be content
to drop in the hand when called.

I try not to feel slighted by those
who refuse; they have mulled it over

and decided to let only the days
lengthen around them, untouched

by gravity and all that it desires,
tightening in their own fragrant heat.

# The Uses of Passion

It has 20/600 vision, because that's all
it needs.
You can find your way anywhere
with it, and will.
It tells you what to wear: a knot *and* a buckle
in the sash of your dress.

It improves your memory.
Eating takes on a whole new meaning.
Confusion becomes a thing of the past; you begin
to make sense of that old riddle
about why the chicken crossed the road. Everything
is much simpler now. You wonder why
you didn't think of this before.

It helps you get up in the morning.
Birds arrive from the forest by the hundreds — all
different species and colors. Without passion,
the woods are struck only by lightning.
With it, the woodsman never has to decide
in which tree his ax belongs.

# After Darwin

The first rule of evolution is that everything must pretend
to be what it's not. So the blind, bald bird flicked
from the nest locks its wings and begins

rowing home, so love turns away
like the blown new moon and becomes indistinguishable
from the nighttime sky.

We are easily moved — as a broken bone
or the blade of a knife, but it's too early in spring
to be traveling away, too early

in the morning while all the tulips
are opening their lips to bees. They remind us
of how we will look at the end: our mouths framed

with parentheses. We say we can do without
directions, and we can, but on this morning in June
between London and Dover, the only track I know

is the one you're riding, and astride these steel haunches
my own steel glides while the hillsides speak
of geometry. The rivers split wide, arch their backs

in abandon, and when the hood of the forest
slips off, exposing the sky, then you see too how the lips
of the rhododendron tremble. Love, we are attached

yet loose, as an eye or a bone in its socket.
Not knowing where we are going, we want only
to arrive: to enter over and over

the way the seven-forty-two slides in again
on time, the way these bones, each morning,
pull into the bank of our bodies like canoes.

# Poems

We know how we like them: good looking and clean cut,
seething, but not too hot. They must be tentative
yet in control, familiar but abandoned.
Like lovers, we want them always new — and faithful.
We admire the firmness of their thighs, but love
the way they turn into what they're not.

Sometimes you go away with them for the weekend
and tossing among sheets in the almost light
tell them dreams you wouldn't dream
of telling anyone else: how the wind was stripping
off bark and boasting of everything it knew,
how it didn't know how the eucalyptus wanted you.

They soon move in and then it's always two steps
forward and a giant step back. They restock
the pantry with foods you can't pronounce, renovate
your appetite and leave crumbs all over the house.
It's just as you imagined, discoveries abound:
poems don't do dishes, but make strudel

you can't do without. One morning they get up and announce
they're moving on. Even after their slow preparations
to leave, the bed is still warm. They say, close
the door quickly: the room will still smell
like us and remember things
neither of us will mention again.

# Nocturne

Shortly after midnight, certain creatures become what they really
Are, bats flex their nostrils and go out to map

The earth with shrieks while slugs outline the borders
Of the real with slime. Possums no longer pretend

To be everything they're not, and for once are just
Possums, while all that's human turns to dream.

Now boundaries realign, and only deer
Know the property lines to my backyard

And whose oak tree it really is.
At this hour nothing stops under street lights

Or for traffic lights for that matter —
Not the deer flicking back the black fleas

Of night, nor I in my sleep, throwing my arm
Across you, as if you weren't there.

## Leaving Phoenix

What was it that turned my eyes blue
that last day in Phoenix, that sent them out

to pierce the night the way an owl snaps
the mouse's spine in two? Each night

the night-blooming cereus solicited
while we slept, uncurling its white flower

to wave at passing bats, but day by day
the rattler scribbled with its hips

in the sand, satisfied to be alone
with just the shape of its sound.

Was it the fence that blooms in spring,
that lineup of ocotillo, impenetrable

delight — or the pincushion cactus, full
of holes, collapsing to the ground

in the heat after sending up
its blossom for an hour like a flag?

Who would have thought that the links
of the cholla would be allowed

to leap at whatever happens by?
And when the barrel cactus, in the rain,

spread its pleats and huffed like a grouse
impressing some mate, why wasn't it arrested

for disturbing the peace? On that last day
in Phoenix, when my eyes finally turned

blue, it was clear that the old law
of the west was gone: comets ricocheted

across the sky until dawn. And whether bold
at noon or lurking by night, the saguaros held up

their arms — stretched out to the sky — giving thanks
or else saying wait, that's enough, we give up.

## Giotto's Last Judgment

Some say that Giotto knew no true perspective
in the Renaissance meaning of the word
because he did not possess the notion

of the infinite. And it's true that in his painting
there is little or no distinction
between the human and the divine.

Still, in the chapel of Scrovegni's palace
on the ruins of the Roman arena,
the Elect are led by the Virgin

in procession, across the inner wall
of the church's facade. In rapture,
they do not know that they are almost

an artistic failure. They couldn't have known
in Pompeii either, after quarreling and deciding again
to sleep apart, where all those evening rehearsals

would lead: assuming their positions,
one knee lifted high, to dream
and then going on unchanged, single file

beneath the ash, in their *pas de chat*
across the courtyard floor. In the fresco
of *The Last Judgment* in Padua,

Giotto's angel of the Apocalypse unfurls
the heavens, which have been standing
behind red drapes in chambers

for centuries, waiting for the cue
to come to bed. And as he rolls up
the wall of the world, the angel explains,

like a used carpet salesman, how passion
first spilled onto life like a stain
and then stayed on indistinguishable

from the color of the fabric itself.
In three-quarters of the picture, the blessed
line up and all look sublime;

in their senior yearbook photos, they gaze
into galaxies and try to find the one
lower quadrant reserved for disarray,

where the damned slide out from heaven
in the loosened henna waves
of God's unpinned hair. Here the lovers,

still reaching, are still full
of flesh; in free fall, they wrangle
but then are snagged at the thigh

by a fist blue and clotted
as a heart. Imperfectly designed
around a troublesome window

on the chapel's entrance wall,
Giotto's fresco lets the angel give
one last pitch: everything,

he continues to insist, reminds us
of something else, points
to something beyond

its own name: the way a spot
on the heart's monitor leaps once
and then lies flat forever

and absence, thin as air,
left alone long enough
turns to flame.

# Notes

**Last Day on Earth in the Eternal City** (2025)

Sometime during 1889 or 1890, Marcel Proust responded to a questionnaire that was popular in France at the time. Proust titled his responses, "Marcel Proust par lui-même" *[Marcel Proust in his own words]*. Some of the topics he responded to are also the titles of the following poems:

*Le don de la nature que je voudrais avoir:* The natural talent I'd like to have
*Ma devise:* My motto
*Le pays où je désirerais vivre:* The country where I want to live

"*Ma devise:*": Walter Benjamin, *The Arcades Project*, [C1a,2].
"When Your Lover Leaves You": The AI sentence is from the essay "The Future of Humanity," composed by OpenAI research institute's GPT-3 natural language processor.
"Shopping List for the Last Day on Earth in the Eternal City": Olga Maslova, *Last Day in the Eternal City* (oratorio).
"Shopping List for Things Now Useless That Recall a Glorious Past": Sei Shōnagon, *The Pillow Book,* 11th Century AD; Galileo Galilei's shopping list, August 1609; Galileo, letter to the Doge of the Republic of Venice, August 24, 1609.

***Parole*** (2018)

"*Lieu de* Moxie *Mémoire*": *Lieux de Mémoire* is Pierre Nora's term for "sites of memory," places and objects that incarnate memory, "where memory crystallizes and secretes itself." Pierre Nora, "Between Memory and History: *Les Lieux de Mémoire*." Gustave Courbet, *The Shelter of the Roe Deer at the Stream of Plaisir-Fontaine, Doubs,* 1866.

"Deep Field": "He telleth the number of the stars ... ," *Psalm* 147:4 KJV; "of all music played on the terraces of the audiences of the moon": Wallace Stevens, "The Figure of the Youth as Virile Poet"; Claude Debussy, *La terrasse des audiences du clair de lune;* Saint Augustine, *Confessions.*

"Nebbiolo": Saint Augustine, *Confessions;* Rhonda K. Garelick, *Mademoiselle: Coco Chanel and the Pulse of History.*

"Beautiful Thinking": Saint Augustine, *Confessions.*

"Parole": "Blue Suede Shoes," as performed by Elvis Presley.

"*La Longue Durée*": Gaston Bachelard, *The Poetics of Space; London's dreadful visitation, or, A collection of all the Bills of Mortality for this present year: beginning the 27th of December 1664, and ending the 19th of December following* ... by Worshipful Company of Parish Clerks, Royal College of Surgeons of England," 1665.

"Fabric": Pierre Nora, "Between Memory and History: *Les Lieux de Mémoire.*"

"Wild. Abandon": "the sky was all 'studied' with stars," Marcel Proust, *In Search of Lost Time,* Vol. IV "Sodom and Gomorrah."

"*Lieu de Moelleux Mémoire*": Shakespeare, *King Lear,* V, ii: "Men must endure/ Their going hence, even as their coming hither;/ Ripeness is all." Bertrand Russell, "'Useless' Knowledge."

"Nice Dark One": Marcel Proust, *In Search of Lost Time,* Vol. VI, "Time Regained."

"*Lieu de* Living *Mémoire*": Carl Safina, *Beyond Words: What Animals Think and Feel.*

*Enchantée* (2013)

"*I Want to Talk About You*": after John Coltrane; Martin Williams, Review of *Africa/Brass* (Impulse! 1961) in *Down Beat;* Dante Alighieri, *The Inferno.*

"History": William James, *The Principles of Psychology;* Elvis Presley, "Love Me Tender."

"*Brief Encounter*": after David Lean's film.

"Note": "drawing near to its desire ... memory cannot follow after it" from Dante Alighieri, *Paradiso.*

"*Item:*": *Belles Heures of Jean de France, Duc de Berry.*

"Shade": David Maisel, *Library of Dust.*

"Ars Poetica": "*E spesso moiano parlando,*" Leonardo da Vinci, in Kenneth D. Keele and Carlo Pedretti, *Leonardo da Vinci: Corpus of the Anatomical Studies in the Collection of Her Majesty the Queen at Windsor Castle.*

"Dessert": Philippe-Alain Michaud, *Aby Warburg and the Image in Motion.*

"Almost Autumn": *God Creating the Stars in an Initial O,* Siena, 15th Century, Wildenstein Collection, Musée Marmottan, Paris.

"Recall": Dante Alighieri, *Purgatorio;* Gaston Bachelard, *The Poetics of Space.*

**Tryst** (2009)

"Takeoff": "*Touch your hair ... the piazza*" from Andrea di Robilant's *A Venetian Affair: A True Tale of Forbidden Love in the 18th Century* (2005).

"*Wrap in Parchment and Also Pink Paper*": Gustaf Sobin, *Luminous Debris: Reflecting on Vestige in Provence and Languedoc* (1999); Cara De Silva, ed. *In Memory's Kitchen: A legacy from the Women of Terezín* (1996).

"*The House in Good Taste*": Elsie de Wolfe, *The House in Good Taste* (1913); Elsie de Wolfe, *After All* (1935).

"First Life of St. Francis": *St. Francis of Assisi: First and Second Life of St. Francis with Selections from the Treatise on the Miracles of Blessed Francis by Thomas of Celano.* trans. Placid Hermann (1988). Book One, Chapter XXIX: 80, 82. Part II epigraph: Michel Gribenski, "*Vers impairs, ennéasyllabe et musique: variations sur un air (mé)connu.*" Joseph Rosenbloom, *The Little Giant Book of Riddles* (1996).

"Tryst": Wendy Goodman and Hutton Wilkinson, *Tony Duquette* (2007).

"It is Virtually Without Thickness and Has Almost": I am indebted to Christopher de Hamel's *Medieval Craftsmen: Scribes and Illuminators* (1992) for lines 1-15. Statue of Diana: discovered during excavations on the site of Jupiter Dolichenus on the Aventine hill in Rome, 1935.

***Chez Nous*** (2005)

"Dance of Ancient Knossos": The italicized lines are performance directions from Erik Satie's *Gnossienne #1* and *#3. Gymnopédies, Gnossiennes and Other Works for Piano,* Dover, 1989.

**Voice-Over** (2002)

"Entrance to an Imaginary Villa": *Villa of P. Fannius Synistor at Boscoreale,* fresco, 40-30 B.C., The Metropolitan Museum of Art; Saint Augustine, *Confessions,* trans. Henry Chadwick (1991); Frances Yates, *The Art of Memory* (1966).

"Scripture": John Ruskin, *The Stones of Venice* (1981); Rudolf Arnheim, "Sculpture: The Nature of a Medium," *To the Rescue of Art* (1992).

"Now and Again: An Autobiography of Basket": Gertrude Stein, "Poetry and Grammar," *Narration* (1935), and *The Autobiography of Alice B. Toklas* (1936). "The Trail of the Lonesome Pine" (Barrad Macdonald and Harry Carroll) was Stein's favorite song. Photograph of Stein and her dog Basket: Gertrude Stein, Paris, 1946, by Horst. ASCOB is an official American Kennel Club designation. Renate Stendhal, *Gertrude Stein in Words and Pictures* (1994).

"Classical Order": 1 Corinthians 13.

"Vermeer Fever": Edward Snow, *A Study of Vermeer* (1994); Lawrence Gowing, *Vermeer* (1970).

"*Amor Ornamenti*": Umberto Eco, *Art and Beauty in the Middle Ages* (1986).

"Narrative": Leonard Barkan, *Unearthing the Past: Archaeology and Aesthetics in the Making of Renaissance Culture* (1999). Rudolf Arnheim, "Negative Space in Architecture," *To the Rescue of Art* (1992). 1 Corinthians 15:52-53.

"*Roma Caput Mundi*": Sigmund Freud, *Civilization and Its Discontents,* trans. James Strachey (1961).

"History": Michelangelo: "By sculpture, I understand an art that takes away superfluous material; by painting, one that attains its result by laying on." Quoted in Mary McCarthy, *The Stones of Florence* (1963). Michelangelo, "Letter to Messer Benedetto Varchi," from Rome, March 1547, in *Michelangelo: Life, Letters, and Poetry,* ed. George Bull (1987).

"The Annunciation in an Initial R": Don Silvestro dei Gherarducci, *The Annunciation in an Initial R,* tempera and gold leaf on parchment, The British Library. Otto Pächt, *Book Illumination in the Middle Ages* (1986).

"*Vedute Da Tempo*": Mary McCarthy, *Venice Observed* (1963). Perry Meisel, "The Unanalyzable." Rev. of *Jacques Lacan,* by Elizabeth Roudinesco. *New York Times Book Review,* April 13, 1997.

"*Trompe l'Oeil*": Leonard Barkan, *Unearthing the Past: Archaeology and Aesthetics in the Making of Renaissance Culture* (1999). E.H. Gombrich, *The Story of Art* (1995). William Blake, "The Book of Thel" (1789).

"More": John Ruskin, *The Stones of Venice* (1981).

**The Uses of Passion** (1995)

"The Uses of Passion": "If a Tree Is Struck by Lightning," Brenda Hillman, *White Dress* (1985).

"After Darwin": Bruce Chatwin, *In Patagonia.*

"Giotto's Last Judgment": Camillo Semenzato, *Giotto* (1964). Eugenio Battisti, *Giotto: Biographical and Critical Study* (1960).

# Acknowledgements

*Last Day on Earth in the Eternal City,* Unbound Edition Press, 2025
*Parole,* Oberlin College Press, 2018
*Enchantée,* Oberlin College Press, 2013
*Tryst,* Oberlin College Press, 2009
*Chez Nous,* Oberlin College Press, 2005
*Voice-Over,* Oberlin College Press, 2002
*The Uses of Passion,* Peregrine Smith Books, Gibbs Smith, Publisher, 1995

*Enchantée* was the winner of the 2015 Kingsley Tufts Poetry Award and the 2014 Audre Lorde Poetry Prize.
*Tryst* was one of two finalists for the 2010 Pulitzer Prize in Poetry.
*Voice-Over* was the winner of the 2001 Alice Fay Di Castagnola Award from the Poetry Society of America and the 2001 FIELD Poetry Prize.
*The Uses of Passion* was the winner of the 1994 Peregrine Smith Poetry Prize.

"Beautiful Thinking" appeared on *Academy of American Poets: Poem-a-Day.*
"Fabric" received the Editor's Prize in Poetry from *Fifth Wednesday.*
"I Want to Talk About You" appeared on *Best American Poetry* online.
"Dark Spots" and "Item:" appeared on *Poetry Daily.*
"Item:" received the 2012 Laurence Goldstein Poetry Prize.
"Wrap in Parchment and Also Pink Paper" also appeared in the anthology *Come Together: Imagine Peace.* Bottom Dog Press, 2008.
"The House in Good Taste" also appeared on *Verse Daily.*
"Elegy," "History," and "Rhapsody" also appeared in *Contemporary Poetry in the United States: A Bilingual English-Cyrillic Edition.* Russia: OGI Press, 2007.

"*Vedute da Tempo*" also appeared in *Gondola Signore Gondola: Venice in 20th Century American Poetry. Venezia:* Supernova, 2007.

"Proverbs" also appeared as a Pushcart Prize selection in *Pushcart Prize XXX,* 2006.

"True Confessions," "Proverbs," "Rendez-Vous" also appeared in *Evensong: Contemporary American Poets on Spirituality,* 2006.

"The Annunciation in an Initial R" and "Now and Again: An Autobiography of Basket" also appeared in *The Extraordinary Tide: New Poetry by American Women,* 2001.

"*Roma Caput Mundi*" also appeared in *Sad Little Breathings & Other Acts of Ventriloquism,* 2001.

"Nocturne" and "Serenade" also appeared in *The Geography of Home: California's Poetry of Place,* 1999.

"Now and Again: An Autobiography of Basket" also appeared in *Queer Dog,* 1997.

Frontispiece and end photos: *Bronze Angel Door Handles* by Emilio Greco, Cathedral of Orvieto, Italy. Photos by Angie Estes.

## About the Author

Angie Estes is the author of seven previous books of poems, most recently *Last Day on Earth in the Eternal City* (Unbound Edition Press). Her book *Enchantée* won the 2015 Kingsley Tufts Poetry Prize and the Audre Lorde Prize for Lesbian Poetry, and *Tryst* was selected as one of two finalists for the 2010 Pulitzer Prize. Her second book, *Voice-Over*, won the 2001 *FIELD* Poetry Prize and was also awarded the 2001 Alice Fay di Castagnola Prize from the Poetry Society of America. Her first book, *The Uses of Passion* (GibbsSmith, 1995), was the winner of the Peregrine Smith Poetry Prize. A collection of essays devoted to Estes's work appears in the University of Michigan Press "Under Discussion" series: *The Allure of Grammar: The Glamour of Angie Estes's Poetry* (2019).

The recipient of many awards, including a Guggenheim Fellowship, a Pushcart Prize and the Cecil Hemley Memorial Award from the Poetry Society of America, she has also received fellowships, grants, and residencies from the National Endowment for the Humanities, the National Endowment for the Arts, the Woodrow Wilson Foundation, the American Academy in Rome, the Lannan Foundation, the California Arts Council, the Illinois Arts Council, and the Ohio Arts Council. In 2023, she was a Writer-in-Residence Fellow at the James Merrill House.

# About the Type and Paper

Designed by Malou Verlomme of the Monotype Studio, Macklin is an elegant, high-contrast typeface. It has been designed purposely for more emotional appeal.

The concept for Macklin began with research on historical material from Britain and Europe dating to the beginning of the 19th century, specifically the work of Vincent Figgins. Verlomme pays respect to Figgins's work with Macklin, but pushes the family to a more contemporary place.

This book is printed on natural Rolland Enviro Book stock. The paper is 100 percent post-consumer sustainable fiber content and is FSC-certified.

*The Swallows Come Out* was designed by Eleanor Safe and Joseph Floresca.

Unbound Edition Press champions honest, original voices. Committed to the power of writers who explore and illuminate the contemporary human condition, we publish collections of poetry, short fiction, and essays. Our publisher and editorial team aim to identify, develop, and defend authors who create thoughtfully challenging work which may not find a home with mainstream publishers. We are guided by a mission to respect and elevate emerging, under-appreciated, and marginalized authors, with a strong commitment to advancing LGBTQ+ and BIPOC voices. We are honored to make meaningful contributions to the literary arts by publishing their work.

unboundedition.com